Trapped by Control

ELLEL MINISTRIES
THE TRUTH & FREEDOM SERIES

Trapped by Control

How to Find Freedom

David Cross

Sovereign World

Sovereign World Ltd
PO Box 784
Ellel
Lancaster LA1 9DA
England

www.sovereignworld.com

ISBN 978 1 85240 501 4

The publishers aim to produce books which will help to extend and build up the Kingdom of God. We do not necessarily agree with every view expressed by the authors, or with every interpretation of Scripture expressed. We expect readers to make their own judgment in the light of their understanding of God's Word and in an attitude of Christian love and fellowship.

Cover design by Andy Taylor
Typeset by Hurix Systems Pvt. Limited
Printed in the United Kingdom

Contents

Introduction

There is a question which every Christian would do well to ask: "Day by day, who or what controls my life?" For many of us, the Lordship of Jesus is continually being challenged by ungodly controls that come from people, situations and even from within ourselves. Control is the foremost motivation behind the spiritual battle that exists in the universe. The desire for authority, and the power to wield that authority, is the primary plan and purpose of Satan, the *ruler of this world* as Jesus calls him.

This enemy of souls needs the participation of man to exercise that authority and bring about the disorder and destruction of God's creation. He actively opposes this creation in rebelling against his Maker.

Our inherently sinful nature draws us naturally into the realm of control, through a desire to promote and protect ourselves, and to minimize the wounding that comes through relationships. Control which ignores the authority of Jesus brings considerable damage into the lives of all those affected. However, authority under the direction of Jesus brings radical restoration.

Ellel Ministries have had the opportunity over the last twenty years to minister to many people caught up in ungodly control. It has taught us to take seriously the clear message given on this subject in the Bible. This book will seek to explain the principles we can learn there. Many of us have experienced the damage of wrong control over their lives, but equally we need to face the fact that many of us have learned to control others in a wrong way.

Through the experiences of life many have come to believe, sometimes unconsciously, that being in control of each situation will be a place of protection. Actually it just destroys relationship. Some have also become experts at controlling their own responses to life, both past and present, only to discover that they have shut down from the truth of real relationship with others and even with God.

Many weekend courses held at Ellel Centers around the world have included this subject. One title frequently used has been *Domination, Manipulation and Control*. It has usually been referred to by the team as the *DMC* course, which happens to be the initials of my full name! I'm not sure that this gives me a particular credibility for writing this book. However, I passionately believe that, if we can understand this subject and know how to find freedom from the damage caused by it, the Body of Christ will find tremendous restoration.

I will look at the meaning of ungodly control, the way it started, the effect it has on us, the relevance of *Jezebel* and how we can bring the whole issue before the Lord for His healing. Chapter 8 has a check list to give an indication of how control might be affecting you. A glance at this chapter might make reading the rest of this book even more necessary! Chapter 9 contains suggestions for how you can pray to receive the freedom and wholeness that God desires for each one of us.

I pray that you will be excited to discover more of God's truth about the issue of control as you read through this book. May the words speak clearly to you and lead you to a new place of healing in Christ Jesus.

What is Control?

Definition

Control is exercising authority and power. When God is the source of this authority it's a place of well-being for His people. The Lordship of Jesus is the very best spiritual government over our lives. However, there's a battle in this world for authority and Satan has gained a significant foothold. He even challenged Jesus with this fact.

> *And he (the devil) led Him (Jesus) up and showed Him all the kingdoms of the world in a moment of time. And the devil said to Him, "I will give you all this domain (authority) and its glory; for it has been handed over to me, and I give it to whomever I wish."*
>
> Luke 4:5-6, NAS

When we use *our* authority to control, it's a process of exerting pressure on someone in order to meet our own desires. Depending on the relationship between ourselves and the one we're controlling, we can force them into believing or doing things contrary to the desires of their heart. Our goal is to over-ride their free will and get our own way.

People exercise this kind of control over individuals, groups and even over themselves. We may be trying to achieve something which seems good to us, but a 'good' result doesn't justify control as a means of getting there. Godly authority, on the other hand, always values free will – the ability to make a choice without pressure.

Ungodly control is very different from establishing godly bound-aries and authority. Where there's godly order and the rightful headship of Jesus, people are released to move into their full des-tiny in relationship with God and the Body of Christ. Jesus dele-gated authority and power to His disciples to bring about the plans and purposes of God. When we're fully *under* godly authority we will fully *exercise* godly authority.

Unfortunately the opposite is also true. The enemy rules in this world through the rebellion of mankind acting against God and in agreement with the spirit of this world. Ungodly control can oper-ate both *over* us and *through* us. It's closely associated with fear and denies the fullness of God's love and purposes in our lives. We par-ticipate in control out of a desire to cope with the places of wound-ing and insecurity which come from our experiences of life. This can mean controlling others or allowing ourselves to be controlled. Fear of people, places and situations affect our choices and turn us away from God's direction. If we exercise authority and power, in a way which hasn't been rightfully delegated to us, it is sin.

Ungodly control can defile every type of relationship. One mar-riage partner can manipulate the other. A business manager can control his staff through intimidation. A group can viciously con-trol one person in a gang rape. One person can quietly manipulate a whole group of people. Have you ever been in a group discussion (even of Christians) where the intimidating silence and body lan-guage of one particular person controlled the whole process of the meeting? Rulers can dominate whole nations. The Bible describes this type of control as being a yoke on the necks of the people, driv-ing them against their will.

> *Your father made our yoke hard; now therefore lighten the hard ser-vice of your father and his heavy yoke which he put on us, and we will serve you.*
>
> 1 Kings 12:4, NAS

In this passage, the people of Israel weren't happy with the con-trol of Rehoboam's father Solomon. They were hoping for more freedom, but it was not to be.

Types of control

The word *domination* comes from the Latin *dominus* which means *master*. It is a direct form of ungodly control frequently using threats or violence. It's usually obvious to all concerned and dependent upon the strength of one person taking advantage of the weakness of another. A bully searches out a victim and uses physical or emotional force to get what he desires. Inevitably, children are particularly vulnerable to this form of control, because of their age and size. Domination is sin, and such injustice builds anger and resentment in the heart of the one abused in this way. Parents should *not* stray into this territory of control, even though there's a need for rightful discipline.

Harsh dictators have the ability to dominate a nation only when they have the support of a corrupt army. In order to control through ungodly authority there always needs to be ungodly power. The power base for Satan's authority is the rebellious demonic realm, which supports him. Later we shall explore the enemy's tactics in his desire to control our lives.

Manipulation (literally meaning *to have a hold on someone else*) is a more subtle form of control in which a careful but unseen strategy is used to change a situation or someone else's will to one's own personal advantage. This form of control is learned over time and grows in skill and power. We can feel emotionally blackmailed by the simplest of phrases expressed in an effective way or at a significant moment. Even the words "I forgive you" can be said in such a way as to impose false guilt on the one receiving the apparent pardon. If we had no awareness of the offence, these tactics can leave us tied, by condemnation, to the one who feels offended.

Terrorism (meaning *an organized system of intimidation*) uses fear as the overt means of control. Violence or the threat of violence has been used throughout history by individuals and groups to get their own way for criminal or political purposes. However much we may want to follow what we believe to be a right course of action, it's very hard to do so when we have been told that the result will be extreme violence, either to ourselves or to those for whom we are responsible.

Terrorism relies on creating an environment which feels unsafe, where something destructive can happen at any moment if we don't appease those seeking to control. We're very familiar with this in the activities of religious fundamentalists around the world at the present time, but some people would say that, in a similar way, it felt unsafe in their family home as a child. If the threat of dad's explosive and violent anger always hung over the family, then control through intimidation was the means of rule in the household. This was terrorism at the family level.

One well-know character from the Bible used all these forms of control so effectively that her name has been used (even by Jesus) to describe particular characteristics of control which are demonically empowered and which actively seek to undermine godly authority. We shall be taking a closer look at this character called Jezebel later in this book.

Ungodly control challenges one of the foundational gifts which God has given to every member of the human race: the freedom to make choices. Let's take an extreme example of control. When there's a loaded gun pointed at our heads, it's very difficult to choose to act in opposition to the one holding the gun. We may not have experienced that kind of situation exactly, but our ability to make choices in our lives may have been seriously restricted by those around us.

Free will

Throughout the Bible we're encouraged to understand that our Heavenly Father wants us to love Him because we have made a personal response to His amazing love for us, not because the relationship was somehow pre-fixed and independent of any choice of ours. There are many passages in which God exhorts His people to make a rightful choice to obey His commands. He's pre-determined a special destiny for all of us, although, sadly, many won't enter into that destiny and enjoy what He has prepared for them. But the heart desire of our Heavenly Father is that none of His creation would be left out of His protection.

The Lord is not slow about His promise, as some count slowness, but is patient towards you, not wishing any to perish but for all to come to repentance.

2 Peter 3:9, NAS

Of course God is Spirit and outside the constraints of time. He has always known that some would say *"yes"* to Him and some would say *"no"*. That doesn't stop the assembly of heaven being overjoyed when any one of us actually makes that life-saving choice and says *"yes"*.

In the same way, I tell you, there is joy in the presence of the angels of God over one sinner who repents.

Luke 15:10, NAS

As he watched out for his prodigal son, the father in Luke chapter 15 seemed to know in his heart that eventually his wayward son would come home, but it was clearly worth a very special party when the decision was actually made by the repentant wanderer.

God makes sure that we know what the choices are with regard to relationship with Him and what the consequences will be when a decision has been made. We can never say to Him that He didn't make it clear how we could benefit from all that He has provided for our well-being. But He leaves us to choose. Every indication of Scripture is that free-will choice is a gift from God to mankind which allows a true, unforced relationship with Him.

I am now giving you the choice between life and death, between God's blessing and God's curse, and I call heaven and earth to witness the choice you make. Choose life.

Deuteronomy 30:19, GNB

If the God of the universe has given mankind the gift of choice in relationship with Him, how important it is that we should value free will in our relationships with each other.

Freedom in right relationships

I am a dad. I remember so well the fun of spending precious days with my young children at our remote farmhouse in the highlands of Scotland. There were always jobs needing to be done, even collecting water from a nearby mountain stream in the early months of our living there. Most days the children loved to join me in all that I was doing, even though their actual ability was often limited. These were days of special relationship simply because the children were choosing to be with their dad rather than being held by my control. Of course that didn't deny the need for discipline and boundaries, but it was important that the necessary constraints were wisely established. A ball and chain may stop someone running away from you but it will never lead to a relationship of love.

Some choices that we make just add interest to each day. For a little child it's important that he learns to make his own choices about which toys to play with, but it's not a life-changing decision. However, for adults, there are choices that carry significant consequences. Some decisions which we make clearly oppose God's commands and He warns us that there is a reaping of what has been sown. A good dad will always help his children to understand the importance of thinking carefully before making important decisions.

> *"Come now, and let us reason together," says the Lord, "Though your sins are as scarlet, they will be as white as snow; though they are red like crimson, they will be like wool. If you consent and obey, you will eat the best of the land; but if you refuse and rebel, you will be devoured by the sword." Truly, the mouth of the Lord has spoken.*
>
> Isaiah 1:18-20, NAS

Our Heavenly Father has made us with the capacity to love Him and to love being with Him. How could He enjoy that special relationship with us if He had somehow forced us or fixed us to respond to Him? Of course He desperately longs for us to make right decisions, but a free-will choice is essential for any true relationship, not least with God Himself.

Even Jesus, who described Himself as the One to whom *all authority* had been given (Matthew 28:18), didn't use that authority to hold onto His followers. When hundreds had left Him because they found the teaching too hard, He gently inquired of the twelve disciples what their choice was in this situation.

> *So Jesus asked the twelve disciples, "And you... would you also like to leave?"*
>
> John 6:67, GNB

How amazing that the King of the universe would give such freedom to His followers. Our free-will response to Him is so important.

The ability to say *"No"*

God has established unchanging foundational spiritual laws for the operation of His creation and for our well-being. To ensure that we benefit from these laws He has given us commands which keep us safe. A warning sign at the edge of a steep cliff is simply there to protect us from the harmful effects of the law of gravity. We have a choice to disobey the warning but it would be foolish. We have a similar choice regarding the commands of God which warn us of the danger of ignoring His spiritual laws. God has not created us to be robots forced to follow Him only in the way we have been programmed. For our love relationship with God to be real, we must be free to say "No!"

Peter said *"No"* three times when asked by a slave-girl if he knew Jesus. His denial of Jesus had been motivated by fear, but God gave him another special chance to say *"Yes"*. Jesus met him at daybreak on a beach and simply asked Peter, "Do you love Me?" This time Peter made a different response and so stepped into the special destiny which God had prepared for him. No doubt there was a big celebration in Heaven that morning.

So when they had finished breakfast, Jesus said to Simon Peter, "Simon, son of John, do you love Me?" He said to Him, "Yes Lord; You know that I love You." He (Jesus) said to him, "Shepherd My sheep."

John 21:15, NAS

The benefit of rightful control and the danger of wrong control

There are many times in our lives when we're only too pleased to be under the rightful control of others in authority. We don't expect the pilot of the airplane, in which we're flying, to walk down the cabin apologizing for being in full control of the flight deck. Having made the choice to put ourselves into his hands we're more than happy that he exercises his full authority with all the wisdom that he possesses. In fact the more the pilot demonstrates that he's in control, the safer we feel. The important issue here is that we recognize that he's a man *in* rightful authority because he's a man *under* rightful authority.

How different from the hijacker who usurps that control by force and demands that we follow his instructions. He has claimed authority rather than it being delegated to him. We didn't have the freedom to choose to put ourselves under this new authority and it's certainly no longer a safe environment. Control is very bad for us when we're in the hands of a terrorist. Control is very good for us when we're in the careful hands of one who's in rightful authority.

From now on, then, you must live the rest of your earthly lives controlled by God's will and not by human desires.

1 Peter 4:2, GNB

Summary

Control can be godly or ungodly, depending on whose authority is in place. It's harmful to us when it undermines our freedom to choose. Free will is a gift of God and essential for true relationship especially with Him.

Ungodly control ranges from the obvious to the subtle, from aggressive domination to hidden manipulation. It's sinful behavior which often develops out of our desire to cope with the wounding and the insecurities which we experience in our lives.

Wrongful control spoils relationships and seriously damages lives. We need to take a closer look at how this happens.

CHAPTER 2

What Harm does Control do?

The thorn in relationships

God created men and women to experience and enjoy relationship with one another. When these relationships are in right order under God, there's amazing potential for His blessing. That rightful order will only be in place if we're able to make a free-will choice to be in godly interdependence with other people. If Jesus is given His rightful position in our human relationships, it's both safe, and indeed empowering, to give of ourselves into relationships in the Body of Christ on earth. Paul describes this ideal situation very simply:

> *And be subject to one another in the fear of Christ.*
>
> Ephesians 5:21, NAS

However, many of us try to avoid being under authority, even godly authority, because we have been wounded by wrongful control in the past. Unfortunately, we're motivated more often by our sinful nature and the insecurity which puts us in fear of being hurt. Even if we're in a place of coming under rightful authority, we may yield with our lips but rebel in our hearts, finding subtle ways of maintaining control over our situation. Wounding from the past may also cause us to control others. Even if given a rightful place of authority, we may feel it necessary to impose our position on those we are leading.

Control issues can weave their way through many relationships like the branch of a thorn bush gripping, tearing and destroying the true peace and effectiveness of God's purposes among His people. The problem may not always be obvious at first but often we become increasingly aware of the lack of real harmony and a growing unfruitfulness in the fellowship of believers. Control deeply defiles God's corporate anointing on the Body of Christ here on earth.

The unseen hold of control

In any ungodly relationship, the physical means of control may be seen by all those involved, but there's always an unseen, spiritual issue behind the visible. The Bible often describes ungodly control as an unseen yoke which takes a grip on individuals and communities, holding them in bondage. Think of animals driven by means of a yoke. They can feel the pressure and know who is master but can't really see the instrument of control on their necks. God clearly sees the problem in the lives of His people and declares the need for release, where the yoke is not from Him.

> *Is this not the fast which I choose, to loosen the bonds of wickedness, to undo the bands of the yoke, and to let the oppressed go free and break every yoke?*
>
> Isaiah 58:6, NAS

The oppression of control has affected the lives of many of us. Behind physical or emotional abuse, past or present, there's a spiritual issue which can remain unresolved and very destructive to our well-being, without the Lord's intervention. This lasting unseen tie in controlling relationships is often called an ungodly soul-tie.

Understanding soul-ties

True relationships involve giving something of ourselves to other people, but this should not lead to our being controlled in a wrong way. Where there's godly order in a relationship the tie may be strong but will not be damaging. Paul describes the unseen ties that exist with those in authority over us. They can be strong and lasting like the bond between a master and his slave. But if we have willingly or unwilling given ourselves to the wrongful control of someone, it will rob us of abundant life.

> *Surely you know that when you surrender yourselves as slaves to obey someone, you are in fact the slaves of the master you obey, either of sin, which results in death, or of obedience, which results in being put right with God.*
>
> Romans 6:16, GNB

Where relationships have involved godly submission, the ties are good and will bless us. Sexual relationships within marriage involve the giving of our whole being to our partner. This is what God intended and gives a safe place for intimate expression and nurture of the sexuality of the husband and the wife. Paul tries to explain how deep this act of submission in marriage really is.

> *A wife is not the master of her own body, but her husband is; in the same way a husband is not the master of his own body, but his wife is.*
>
> 1 Corinthians 7:4, GNB

The problem comes when this surrender of our whole being happens outside the covenant of marriage. In this case, we give ungodly control over our body to our sexual partner. We create unseen but lasting and destructive ties. Sexual relationships outside marriage may be described by the world as *casual*, but the lasting spiritual effect is certainly *not* casual. Many who have been involved in occult or satanic activity know the substantial power of control that can be established through sexual intercourse.

Wrongful control of any sort establishes ungodly soul-ties. The control can be from physical, emotional or spiritual roots. These destructive ties are places of spiritual darkness and can be used and empowered by the enemy. Praise God that this bondage can be

broken as we bring the controlling relationships of the past before
the Lord for His cleansing. We shall look at the steps to freedom
in chapter 9.

The damage to the individual

Many of the religious leaders around Jesus were masters of control.
They made strict rules and regulations which held the people in a
place of oppression and intimidation. Ungodly control can weigh
very heavily on the whole of our being.

> *They tie up heavy burdens and lay them on men's shoulders, but they
> themselves are unwilling to move them with so much as a finger.*
> Matthew 23:4, NAS

God didn't design our bodies to carry such a load. It crushes the
human soul and the human spirit, eventually bringing disorder to
our physical being. Our bodies will always reflect the condition of
our hearts.

I remember a man we will call Graham, who told us about his
childhood. His memory of his mother was that he had lived continually under her disapproval. It seemed as if every day he had
tried to please her, but almost never heard words of affirmation or
encouragement. He led his life tied to a desperate hope for mum's
approval, increasingly weighed down by her negative responses.
I have seldom seen a man so clearly bent over by such relentless
control. His physical stoop was very pronounced.

As we talked, he began to forgive his mother and to declare his
desire to walk in freedom. He began to recognize, for the first time,
just how much God approved of His children, not least Graham.
We asked the Lord to lift the spiritual yoke of disapproval from
his mother who had exercised control over him for so long. The
result was immediately visible. His face changed from displaying
pain to relief. He stretched his neck and head and declared that a
huge weight had lifted from him. He walked out of the room with
a completely different stature. Control significantly oppresses lives
but God actively desires our freedom.

Taking control

We're not just damaged by coming *under* ungodly control. We harm ourselves when we let control operate *through* us. When we assume control beyond what has been rightfully delegated to us, we move into an area which is likely to be very stressful for ourselves. A soldier who has been given, and is following, the clear orders of his commanding officer may well experience a hard battle but there's a security for him. He's operating within the boundaries of his mission. It would be very different if he decided to take charge of the whole battle field. He would need to try to assess all the maneuvers of the enemy and his allies. He would soon be overwhelmed and the result would be a disaster.

Some people spend every day of their lives trying to control everything and everyone around them to try to bring a sense of security or significance to the troubled places within them. For many, this has gone on for so long that it's become a way of life, although they aren't conscious of it. Such control is exhausting and eventually overloads the body. God didn't design us to run His world single-handed, not even the bit of it that surrounds us!

We are meant to find a right place of interdependence with those around us, sometimes leading, and sometimes following, as the Spirit of God enables us. In the Body of Christ, a godly leader should simply *offer* direction to those for whom he's responsible. If he *demands* to be followed, the outcome will be defiled by his control. As with the followers of Jesus, when He walked the earth, people must be free to say *"No"*, even if it's not a wise choice.

The relationship between our spirit, soul and body

Our human soul is comprised of our mind, our emotions and in particular our will, the place where decisions are made day by day. God intended that the directing of these choices would be through the wisdom, which He imparts to us through our human spirit.

But it is a spirit in man, and the breath of the Almighty gives them understanding.

Job 32:8, NAS

Our human spirit has been part of our being from conception. For those of us who receive Jesus, there's a birth of our spirit from a place of darkness into a place of spiritual light, which brings us into a new opportunity to know the truth and the wisdom of God. We begin to *see* God's viewpoint, for the first time.

As disciples of Jesus our soul faces an important choice every moment of the day. We can follow the direction given by our human spirit, which is being led by the Holy Spirit, or let our sinful nature take control, so that we end up following the ways of this world. In effect, our soul makes the decision as to who or what controls our lives. These choices can bring spiritual life or spiritual death to the whole body.

Ignoring the leading of the Spirit of God is sometimes called *'soulish'* behavior. It's as if the soul within us stands up, presses down on our human spirit and declares that it's taken control! It can seem like the only solution in a crisis but it's not dissimilar to the hijacker on a plane over-riding the authority of the pilot. Order, safety and right direction are lost. Disaster is likely to be the outcome. We can also call this way of behaving 'ungodly self-control'.

This *'soulish'* control is very different from the self control listed as a fruit of the Spirit in Galatians 5:23. Later we'll explore in detail the issue of how we control our own lives in both right and wrong ways. The order within our being between the human spirit, the soul and the body has been designed by God to protect and provide for our lives in an amazing way. When this order is destroyed through ungodly control or *'soulish-ness'* it brings dysfunction and distress into every part of our being. Jesus knows that we desperately need a rightful spiritual authority directing our souls. He knows all about damaging yokes. It's always best when He's in charge.

Come to Me, all who are weary and heavy-laden, and I will give you rest. Take My yoke upon you and learn from Me, for I am gentle and humble in heart, and you will find rest for your souls.

Matthew 11:28-29, NAS

Wrongful control defiles every aspect of our lives. It can affect our relationships in the family, in the church and at work. For many of us, we have learned to live with it, work around it and deal with it in many different ways. Perhaps it is now time to *confront* it, both in our own lives and in the lives of our brothers and sisters in Christ. We may spend much time diagnosing and removing the virus in our computer. However, the disorder and damage caused by control in our relationships often goes unchallenged. Truthfully living as part of God's Kingdom means pruning the dead wood, which is unfruitful and brings disease into the vine. Controlling behavior is certainly 'dead wood'.

The enemy empowers ungodly control

Obedience to God's commands gives the Holy Spirit authority in our lives. God's commandments have now been expressed for us under the new covenant in a very succinct way.

This is His commandment, that we believe in the name of His Son Jesus Christ, and love one another, just as He commanded us.

1 John 3:23, NAS

Controlling behavior is *not* loving behavior. Disobeying God's commands gives spiritual authority to the enemy, who has been given control over the kingdoms of this world through the rebellion of mankind.

Exercising ungodly control plays right into the enemy's hands because it actively extends his sphere of influence. Later when we take a closer look at the story of Jezebel, we will see that her progressive desire to control became demonically inspired.

When Joram saw Jehu, he said, "Is it peace Jehu?" And he answered, "What peace, so long as the harlotries of your mother Jezebel and her witchcrafts are so many?"

2 Kings 9:22, NAS

Controlling power, exercised through someone operating outside God's authority, is indeed 'witchcraft'. Covenant relationship with God is broken and the control lies within the enemy's domain. Such destructive control is not just a *characteristic* of Satan and his kingdom of darkness, it's his *purpose*. As much as God's Kingdom is bonded together through love, Satan's domain is held in bondage through intimidation. His domain controls through fear. Of course the realm of darkness is not equal in any way to God's Kingdom of light, but the demonic realm remains desperate to hang on to whatever authority is permitted by man's sin. Ungodly control gives the enemy rights.

The people of the early church in Galatia were allowing themselves to be increasingly controlled by all sorts of religious and legalistic practices. Paul warned them of the demonic spiritual consequence.

But now that you know God, or I should say now that God knows you, how is it that you want to turn back to those weak and pitiful ruling spirits? Why do you want to become their slaves all over again? You pay special attention to certain days, months, seasons, and years. I am worried about you! Can it be that all my work for you has been for nothing?

Galatians 4:9-11, GNB

The seduction of control

The ability to exercise supernatural control over other people can be very attractive for those struggling with rejection and insignificance. When we have apparently had so little influence in our relationships, it can seem important to get our own way. Some people gradually experience an increasing supernatural ability as they practice control. If occult rituals are added, the empowering can take on a sinister aspect.

Some while ago we were praying for a lady, let's call her Susan, who confessed that, before becoming a Christian, she had gone through an occult ritual with a New Age practitioner. The purpose had been to seek the power of control in her relationships with men. The ritual had in fact involved sacrifice of a small animal and the result had been amazingly effective. She looked back with deep contrition and horror at what she had done but she knew it was now time to receive God's forgiveness. As we asked the Lord to release her from the controlling powers, she went through deep deliverance and found a place of freedom and even physical healing.

The story of Harry Potter is about a boy who finds himself able to move out of his world of insignificance through the discovery of an occult power to control others. It may be a fictional story but it actively embraces and reflects the actual world of witchcraft. How sad that so many children are not finding their true value and destiny in a supernatural relationship with Jesus.

Through the degrees of membership in Freemasonry, vows and oaths are spoken and rituals are enacted, involving many parts of the human body. In effect demonic authority is being invited into those rituals and ceremonies. The participants are actively submitting their bodies to the control of the powers of darkness. As we have prayed with men who have renounced the vows, oaths and rituals, we have seen that such control over the physical body has frequently led to disorder and infirmity. Whether we take control or submit to control in ways that disobey God, there can be opportunity for spiritual bondage to affect and damage our lives.

The enemy is seductive and deceptive. His primary aim is to gain control through our sinful beliefs and behaviors. When control is not in the hands of God it's in the hands of the kingdom of darkness. We need to take seriously the effect that wrongful control has had on individuals and families.

Summary

Ungodly control affects every part of our being. Whether we are the object of control or the perpetrator of control it can be equally damaging. The human body was designed to experience godly authority through being led by the Spirit of God. We weren't designed to be vessels for ungodly control. It puts our bodies into spiritual distress and darkness. The physical body will in some way always display the effect of this inner disorder.

Wrongful control in relationships can establish unseen but lasting ties which hold us in bondage to those with whom we've had relationship. Soul ties pull us away from the One who wants to be the true Master of our lives. He longs to set us free from these damaging yokes.

Ungodly control is enemy territory. Where, through man's sin, he has been given authority to operate over us or through us, he can empower that right demonically. Unclean spirits promote driven-ness in our thoughts, decisions and actions. The enemy has always desired that we would give him control.

CHAPTER 3

What's Wrong with Authority and Power?

Who is holding the dynamite?

Authority and power are an essential part of our existence. The problem comes when the person in control is not operating in accordance with God's order. To exercise control in any situation we need to have *authority*, which gives the *right* to act. We also need *power* which gives the *ability* to act. If the authority has not been rightfully delegated to us then we are assuming a right to operate by our *own* authority, which can lead to serious problems.

Let's look at the example of a manager of a rock quarry. He has been delegated the authority, by the owners of the land, to remove rock from the quarry and to sell it to road contractors for building embankments. He is in charge of operations in the quarry and has been given full *authority* to carry out the task. But just having authority is not enough. He needs also the ability or *power* to carry out the task. The most important item of power which he needs is dynamite! Tough rock cannot be removed from the quarry without it.

Provided that he uses the dynamite within the boundaries of his authority, the job can be carried out safely and to the benefit of all concerned. But what if he secretly decides to take the dynamite home to create a pond in his garden? He has plenty of power in his hands but he is not under right authority. In fact he has assumed his *own* authority. The consequence could well be disastrous.

Interestingly, in the New Testament, the Greek word which is translated as *authority* is *exousia*, from which we get words like executive. The Greek word which is translated as *power* is *dunamis*, from which we get words like dynamite. It is important that we recognize the difference between these terms and the significance of rightful and wrongful authority.

The need for safe hands

Authority and power are essential for God's plans and purposes through the Body of Christ. When Jesus sent out the first twelve disciples to begin the work on His behalf, it's clearly recorded that they were acting under His delegated authority and that they were effective in their ministry because He directly empowered them.

> *And He [Jesus] called the twelve together, and gave them power and authority over all the demons and to heal diseases.*
>
> Luke 9:1, NAS

In the verses which follow, Jesus gives them detailed instructions and boundaries within which to operate. As long as they remained in obedience to His instructions and therefore under His authority, they experienced His power, as it was needed, to enter the spiritual battle.

In the book of Acts, we are reminded of the danger of trying to exercise spiritual power when not under rightful authority.

> *Some Jews who traveled around and drove out evil spirits also tried to use the name of the Lord Jesus to do this. They said to the evil spirits, "I command you in the name of Jesus, whom Paul preaches."*
>
> *Seven brothers, who were the sons of a Jewish High Priest named Sceva, were doing this. But the evil spirit said to them, "I know Jesus, and I know about Paul; but you, who are you?" The man who had the evil spirit in him attacked them with such violence that he*

overpowered them all. They ran away from his house, wounded and with their clothes torn off.

Act 19:13-16, GNB

The kingdom of darkness possesses considerable demonic power. This power can be manifested when man is in disobedience to God's laws and commands. Jesus gave the disciples a simple picture to help them understand the significance and safety of being fully under His authority.

Behold, I have given you authority to tread on serpents and scorpions, and over all the power of the enemy, and nothing will injure you.

Luke 10:19, NAS

I had a particular example of the truth of these Scriptures recently. I was in India attending a ceremony to lay the foundation stone for a proposed Christian healing Center. As the ground was being dug, one of the workmen, who were bare-footed, was bitten by a poisonous scorpion. We claimed the truth of the verse above and sought the Lord's protection and healing. The workman was unaffected by the poison. Praise God!

Right authority is delegated, defined and it brings order

When we come upon a traffic accident, we are only too pleased when a policeman arrives to take control. We can see by his uniform that he's someone under right authority and we expect that he's acting within right boundaries in dealing with such a situation. He's empowered by the training which he has received and also the equipment which he carries, such as radios, sirens and flashing lights. His control does us no harm. In fact it brings order and restoration to a difficult situation.

Before being released to patrol the streets, the policeman has been given clear instructions on what he's permitted to do and what equipment he's permitted to use. He's a man *exercising* right

authority because he's a man *under* right authority. Jesus was just
the same, but it took a Roman military officer to fully recognize
this fact. A centurion was one day seeking healing for his servant
so he sent friends to ask Jesus for help. He told them to ask Jesus
just to speak out the healing, for he recognized the authority which
had been invested in Jesus.

> *So Jesus went with them. He was not far from the house when the*
> *officer sent friends to tell Him, "Sir, don't trouble Yourself. I do*
> *not deserve to have You come into my house, neither do I consider*
> *myself worthy to come to You in person. Just give the order, and*
> *my servant will get well. I, too, am a man placed under the author-*
> *ity of superior officers, and I have soldiers under me. I order this*
> *one, 'Go!' and he goes; I order that one, 'Come!' and he comes; and*
> *I order my slave, 'Do this!' and he does it." Jesus was surprised*
> *when He heard this; He turned around and said to the crowd fol-*
> *lowing Him, "I tell you, I have never found faith like this, not even*
> *in Israel!"*
>
> Luke 7:6-9, GNB

We are told in John chapter 8 that Jesus only did what the Father
told him to do. Jesus was able to exercise extraordinary supernatural authority and power because He operated strictly under
the direction of the Father. The centurion officer recognized the
military equivalent and Jesus was amazed at his perception and
trust. If even Jesus has determined to use His power only under
the Father's authority, then we, as His Body on earth, should take
very careful note. We truly represent Jesus only when we're in a
relationship with Him of complete submission.

> *So He said to them, "When you lift up the Son of Man, you will*
> *know that 'I Am Who I Am'; then you will know that I do nothing*
> *on my own authority, but I say only what the Father has instructed*
> *me to say.*
>
> John 8:28, GNB

The safety of power depends on the source of the authority

Sometimes in Christian meetings we see exciting, powerful and supernatural occurrences. It's easy in this very secular world to assume that when we see something supernatural, it must be God's work that we're witnessing. It's true that the gifts of the Holy Spirit are manifestations of God's power and that we should earnestly desire these gifts in a world which desperately needs healing from brokenness and bondage. But Jesus warns us that we should look out for what might be false by questioning the fruit that we see.

The Spirit of God seeks to grow good fruit in our lives. In fact this fruit (described in Galatians 5:22-23) is quite simply the unique character of Jesus. It's not the degree of power but the development of this good fruit which gives us certainty that the authority of Jesus is in place. Without the appearance of the right fruit, there is doubt over whose authority, and therefore whose power, is being displayed.

> *Beware of the false prophets, who come to you in sheep's clothing, but inwardly are ravenous wolves. You will know them by their fruits.*
>
> Matthew 7:15-16, NAS

If the character of Jesus is not evident and growing, we need to suspect that the power, at least in part, is coming from an enemy source. The good fruit of the Holy Spirit declares that the authority of Jesus is in place. In the safety of this authority, the gifts of the Holy Spirit truly declare His power.

Control is the result of exercising authority and power. Jesus brought into this world a radically new form of control, which if totally centered on Him and His ways, results in liberty and healing for mankind. He knew that He was completely contradicting the ways in which control was being used by those in authority in the world.

Jesus called them to Himself and said, "You know that the rulers of the Gentiles lord it over them, and their great men exercise authority over them. It is not this way among you, but whoever wishes to become great among you shall be your servant, and whoever wishes to be first among you shall be your slave; just as the Son of Man did not come to be served, but to serve, and to give His life a ransom for many."

Matthew 20:25-28, NAS

The experience of control from childhood to adulthood

From the moment of birth we have experienced control. A newborn child is utterly helpless, so God entrusted our parents with complete authority over our lives for our protection and provision. We were literally held tightly by them for our comfort and our safety. If this was done in godly ways, their control over our lives was entirely good for us. Of course our parents weren't perfect and godly control is easily defiled by sin.

As we grew and began walking, every step could take us into danger. The wisdom and control of our parents remained essential for our well-being. Our immature choices sometimes needed to be overridden by parents to keep us from danger. However, the training of our will was equally important. Sometimes we needed to experience the consequence of wrong (but not harmful) personal choices. If the freedom to choose was never permitted, the control over our lives wasn't as God intended.

As we matured in body and mind, God also desired that we would be strengthened in our human spirit. John the Baptist was clearly loved and affirmed by his parents. We are briefly told of how he grew into maturity and reliance upon God.

The child grew and developed in body and spirit. He lived in the desert until the day when he appeared publicly to the people of Israel.

Luke 1:80, GNB

God wants us to learn how to be directed by Him, the ultimate authority, by first learning from the godly leading of our parents. Children need clear direction, clear boundaries and a clear understanding of the consequences of rebellion, all within a safe learning environment. It's only by being allowed to make mistakes that children learn to make right decisions. The day-to-day control of parents needs to diminish as children discover how to make their own choices and hopefully come to know the personal guidance of Jesus.

Children need to be gently picked up when they have fallen, not put in fear of ever getting it wrong. Sadly, the harsh control of many parents has crushed the spirit of their children, sowing anger and defensive control into young hearts.

Fathers, do not provoke your children to anger, but bring them up in the discipline and instruction of the Lord.

Ephesians 6:4, NAS

However much parents may want to protect their children, their task is to train them so that, at some point, they can be entirely released from parental control and have the confidence to make their own life choices. There comes a time when parents must fully release their children. This would normally be when they leave home or get married. Parents needn't ever stop praying for their children or being available for advice and help, but God intended that, at the right time, *all* control must cease. Jesus reminds us of the significance of this when someone gets married. Without a complete *leaving* there will never be a complete *cleaving* (uniting).

And God said, 'For this reason a man will leave his father and mother and unite with his wife, and the two will become one.'

Matthew 19:5, GNB

Adult relationships should involve godly submission to one another, but never wrongful control. When there's right authority and right order, God's spiritual covering protects and blesses our relationships. When we lose right order in marriage, families, churches and nations, through control and selfishness, we expose our lives to the enemy's rule and hostility. We shall take a look, in the last chapter, at how God views leadership within His Body on earth.

Summary

Authority is the *right* to do something. Power is the *ability* to do it. Together they become control. When this is being exercised in godly order through right delegation and within right boundaries, authority and power bring protection and purpose.

We can be sure that the authority of Jesus is in place when the good fruit of the Holy Spirit is evident and growing in the lives of those involved. When the authority is right, the power is safe. This power is manifested through the supernatural gifts of the Holy Spirit enabling the Body of Christ to bring freedom and wholeness into a damaged world.

However there's also an enemy at work in this world who gains spiritual authority through the sinfulness of mankind. When we assume authority outside God's order we empower this enemy to disrupt and destroy relationships and bring damage to individual lives. It's been this way from the beginning of the world.

CHAPTER 4

Why do People Control?

Authority at creation

At the very moment of the creation of mankind, God chose to delegate to men and women spiritual authority over all the earth and all the animals.

> *God blessed them; and God said to them, "Be fruitful and multiply, and fill the earth, and subdue it; and rule over the fish of the sea and over the birds of the sky and over every living thing that moves on the earth."*
>
> Genesis 1:28, NAS

The word translated *subdue* literally means to *stand on*. God was telling mankind that he was to go and claim authority over the earth by walking on it. God had given man an amazing destiny to manage the earth on behalf of his Maker. Such enormous authority needed clear boundaries. God gave an instruction to man that he was to trust that God knew best how to direct His creation in all that was right and wrong.

> *The Lord God commanded the man, saying. "From any tree of the garden you may eat freely; but from the tree of the knowledge of good and evil you shall not eat, for the day that you eat from it you will surely die."*
>
> Genesis 2:16-17, NAS

Man was given extraordinary authority, together with power to demonstrate God's fruitfulness in His creation. He was also given the necessary instructions for remaining safe in this amazing adventure. Man was to be *under* God's control in order to be rightfully *in* control of the created world. But man was also given a free will to say *'No'*.

Problems in the Garden

All sinful behavior has its origin in the disobedience and rebellion of our first forebears, Adam and Eve, who were tempted away from a relationship of obedience with God. It's clear from Scripture that Satan was created a powerful being but he has eternally lost his place of authority in heaven, through rebellion.

> *Then war broke out in heaven. Michael and his angels fought against the dragon, who fought back with his angels; but the dragon was defeated, and he and his angels were not allowed to stay in heaven any longer. The huge dragon was thrown out, that ancient serpent, named the Devil, or Satan, that deceived the whole world. He was thrown down to earth, and all his angels with him.*
>
> Revelation 12:7-9, GNB

In the Garden of Eden, the serpent sees an opportunity for regaining a realm of authority, if he can get man to follow him. It's a foundational truth that when we follow an instruction, we give authority over our lives to the instructor. When Adam and Eve disobeyed God and agreed with the direction of Satan, the spiritual authority which God had invested in man was handed over to the devil.

> *And the devil led Jesus up and showed Him all the kingdoms of the world in a moment of time. And the devil said to Him, I will give you all this domain (authority) and its glory; for it has been handed over to me, and I give it to whomever I wish.*
>
> Luke 4:5-6, NAS

Jesus didn't contradict this statement. However He *did* refuse to do the same as every other man who has walked the earth; he did *not* follow the ways of this world nor the instructions of its ruler.

From the moment that our first forebears followed the instruction of Satan, it became a battle for control over the soul of man. God had given man clear instructions for his well-being but He also gave man a free will to obey God or to rebel against Him. God's desire has always been that we would dwell in peace under His direction, but when Adam and Eve followed the deceptive instruction of Satan, they chose independence from God. They stepped out of the safety of His authority and power, and entered into the exposed and hostile spiritual domain of the powers of darkness. It was clearly very uncomfortable.

> *As soon as they had eaten it, they were given understanding and realized that they were naked; so they sewed fig leaves together and covered themselves.*
>
> Genesis 3:7, GNB

In this place of spiritual vulnerability they felt naked and fearful. It was then that ungodly control was sown into the history of man as they further decided that they would cover themselves, without God's authority. Separated from their Maker, it just seemed the best thing to do. Surely, they thought, someone had to take control of the situation? All mankind has followed the same argument ever since. Fear is a major motivator for control.

> *But the LORD God called out to the man, "Where are you?"*
>
> *He answered, "I heard you in the garden; I was afraid and hid from you, because I was naked."*
>
> Genesis 3:9-10, GNB

From bad to worse

The control issues in this first family were destined to deteriorate rapidly. Separation from the safety of God's spiritual covering inevitably led to insecurity, distrust, disorder and the need to find ways of coping, frequently through control in relationships and not least in families.

> *To the woman He said, "I will greatly multiply your pain in child-birth, in pain you will bring forth children; yet your desire will be for your husband, and he will rule over you."*
>
> Genesis 3:16, NAS

It wasn't long before the desire to control reached an extreme in the relationship between Cain and Abel. Insecurity and rejection can lead us to strong responses of ungodly control against those whom we perceive as a threat. It can sometimes lead to intense hatred and even murder. This family feud was no longer the fruit of God's character being displayed on earth but the destructive character of a new *ruler of the world*, a title which Jesus Himself would give to Satan.

This spiritual ruler only gets his authority on earth through the rebellion of man. When we step out of godly order, authority and power we enter the enemy's territory and give him an increasing right to exercise his demonic power both against us and through us. Ungodly control isn't just bad behavior, it's fuel for the powers of darkness, as we shall see clearly when we look at the life of Jezebel.

Control is part of our defiled inheritance

Once the issue of ungodly control was sown into the history of mankind at the Fall, it inevitably became a part of our own sinful nature. We unfortunately carry a tendency to protect ourselves from the painful issues of life by using tools such as control.

If I'm insecure because I've been rejected or wounded by others, I'll desire to control my environment, and other people, in order to try to feel safe. I may also desire to control how I present myself to others, in order to avoid rejection and to become what I consider acceptable to those around me. Ungodly control always appears where there's an absence of godly authority. When leaders fail to give clear direction it causes those following to try to fill the void. Weak husbands invite dominating wives. Harsh husbands invite deceptive and manipulative wives. God has shown us His order in families and in churches. Some are called to give godly direction to others, but where they fail to follow God's guidelines, they open a door to wrong control.

Control can be a characteristic weakness in the family line. Parents and grandparents may have adopted a life-style of control as a consequence of their own wounding. This pattern of control is out of line with God and can get passed from generation to generation through learned behavior as well as the spiritual principle of generational iniquity. In fact the word which is translated as *iniquity* in the Old Testament means *crookedness* or being *out of line*. The passing down in families of this type of disorder in relationships is exactly what the Bible warns us of, where there has been rebellion against God's authority in our forebears.

> *You shall not worship them [other gods] or serve them; for I, the Lord your God, am a jealous God, visiting the iniquity of the fathers on the children, on the third and the fourth generations of those who hate Me.*
>
> Exodus 20:5, NAS

When children have experienced ungodly control in the family, they not only learn to control others but they become fearful of being controlled by anyone in authority. They unconsciously develop these attitudes, which very often lead to issues of rebellion and independence. I remember talking to a lady recently who remembered, as a little girl, once seeing the full extent of her dad's anger. It was such a frightening experience that she spent the rest of her childhood trying to manipulate situations in the family in an attempt to avoid a repeat of the explosion. In effect, dad's control, through the threat of anger, had led to her trying to control everyone around her just to keep the peace.

Everyone is doing it!

The world is full of controlling relationships. Many of us are totally unaware of the ways in which *we* manipulate situations and people in order to protect the insecure feelings within. The Bible encourages us to avoid association with those who display aggressive behavior; otherwise we will learn their ways.

> *Don't make friends with people who have hot, violent tempers. You might learn their habits and not be able to change.*
> Proverbs 22:24-25, GNB

It is not always easy to avoid them! However, God calls us to be *in* the world but not *of* it. We are called to be different in how we seek significance and safety in all our relationships. The Lordship of Jesus makes it possible to see authority and power in a completely new way.

He didn't just bring a teaching to make us behave better; Jesus brought the Kingdom of God down to earth. In this amazing Kingdom, domination, manipulation and intimidation aren't part of any relationship.

Jesus, the One to whom *all* authority has been given, even washed the feet of His disciples while giving them clear commands how to follow His example. He demonstrated that exercising godly authority and power does not mean crushing others. In fact it means strengthening others and nurturing them in the depth of their human spirit.

Children can and do control their parents

I was recently listening to a radio program about a 5-year old girl who had been adopted by a couple. The little girl had experienced horrendous abuse before coming to them. The adoption seemed to start well but step by step the little girl began to exercise extraordinary control over the family including the couple's son, who was of toddler age.

The parents, who were not Christians, described the never-ending intensity of the situation in the household. The little adopted girl demanded attention every moment of the waking day and used increasingly sinister techniques to control the family. She seemed to desperately want their love but at the same time to push the family into destruction. She constantly provoked each of them with hurtful words and behaviors. She even said to the parents that a little voice inside her was telling her to work against them.

The family received no help from social services as they couldn't understand why it had seemed to go so wrong. Eventually the adoption failed, the little girl returned to institutional care, and the couple separated. The radio program offered no understanding of the spiritual significance of all that had happened, but it was so clear that the enemy had used a desperately wounded child to gain a place of control and division in an ordinary well-meaning family.

The enemy is always prowling

Because any ungodly control gives authority to the enemy, he will forever be trying to deceive us into believing that a little control will smooth the rough road ahead. He certainly tried it with Jesus. Until the Son of Man walked the earth, Satan had always found ways of exercising his control through sinful human lives.

In His time of testing in the wilderness, Jesus was challenged by Satan to ignore the authority of Father God and follow the advice of this worldly ruler. Had He wanted to, Jesus had limitless ability to take control of the situation and ease His difficult journey on earth. However, He chose to remain under the Father's direction and therefore was able to walk with undefiled authority and power into His destiny.

I thank Jesus that He loved each one of us too much to take the easy way out. In Christ, we have an amazing opportunity to have His attitudes within us, knowing and displaying both His authority and his servant-heart.

Unfortunately the enemy will not stop looking for opportunities to empower his control over us and through us. For example, we looked earlier at the issue of anger in the father of a family. Unresolved anger from some injustice of the past lies in the hearts of many people. It may be well buried but can occasionally explode into violent activity, intimidating and controlling those who happen to be in the vicinity. The enemy can use this unhealed issue, which lies in spiritual darkness, to stir up relational discord.

> *An angry man stirs up strife, and a hot-tempered man abounds in transgression.*
>
> Proverbs 29:22, NAS

Every follower of Jesus soon discovers that he's in a spiritual battle. The battle is for control of the human heart. If we choose to abandon ungodly control, in obedience to Jesus, we find that the Holy Spirit both governs and empowers our lives to relate to others with confidence and safety. When we permit sinful behaviors, such as control, to operate in us and through us we give rule to the enemy who can then use the demonic realm to drive us further into his grip. We need to be alert to the way the enemy gets the upper hand through ungodly control.

> . . . *so that no advantage would be taken of us by Satan, for we are not ignorant of his schemes.*
>
> 2 Corinthians 2:11, NAS

Summary

We try to control others and ourselves because we believe it will stop us getting hurt. Sometimes we do it to try to give ourselves significance, power or security. In fact it doesn't work because wrong control defiles relationships and only leads to deception, isolation and further rejection. Others may submit to our intimidation but we will never have a heart-felt relationship with them.

The roots of control were in the Garden of Eden as our first forebears chose to take control, first in rebellion and then in trying to resolve their nakedness. Sowing fig leaves together was an act of independence. In effect, they said to themselves, "We've got a problem but don't worry; we have got it under control!"

The enemy seeks to take advantage of any area of ungodly control in order to further his authority in this rebellious world. We need revelation from the Lord to show us the truth of our attitudes and behaviors, where control has found its way into our lives. Jesus is ready and willing to shine His light into any darkness and release us from its grip.

CHAPTER 5

How do People Control?

Working on the emotions

We learn the art of control from a very young age. At the time of writing this book, my own grandchildren are all under the age of five and they're just lovely. However they have very inventive abilities when it comes to pressing on the tender emotions of their grandparents. Trying to get their own way with soft targets like us just seems to come naturally to them. It's so interesting to see that when godly boundaries are put back in place by their mum and dad we see the children at peace with the right authority over their lives.

Emotional blackmail is a well *known* phrase simply because it is a well *used* form of control. It's of course used most effectively on people who care about us. The method is to make it clear to them that we will suffer great pain unless they fall in with our point of view. We seek to control their choices towards us through the route of their compassion. We can try a range of tactics from tears to temper tantrums, from a pained expression to the extremes of suicidal threats. If others are watching we can even try embarrassing our target in front of the shocked spectators.

It's amazing how a particular emphasis in our words can just hook into the conscience of the one we're seeking to control. "You go and enjoy yourself; I'll be alright here on my own." When said by an experienced manipulator, these words contain the unspoken threat of almost certain mishap for the one so cruelly left alone.

The issue of right and wrong responsibility and dependence is very important. We mustn't get wrongfully tied to our friends and family, even the most needy of them. To love them and care for them is good within right boundaries, but we mustn't replace Jesus as their savior.

Fear – the ultimate controller

Probably the most direct way to govern the will of another person is through causing them to be in fear. Fear is a God-given emotion that's intended to motivate us. It motivates us to make choices to avoid danger either to ourselves or to those we are responsible for. Terrorism is the most extreme use of fear to exercise control. By threatening violence to us or our loved-ones, the terrorist can control us most effectively. However, in our daily lives intimidation can also be common. Fear of rejection, fear of ridicule, fear of exposure, fear of disapproval can all be used against us by a clever opponent seeking to influence our decisions for their own benefit.

Several times I have mentioned that the use of anger, or the threat of anger, can be a powerful weapon in the hands of someone seeking to control. Buried anger is just like the molten magma below a volcano which seems to be dormant. When it does eventually spew out on those dwelling nearby, it can be highly destructive. We're happy to do anything that might avoid such an eruption. Many people at their place of work get used to appeasing the boss in order to avoid such an eruption. When we appease in this way we're actually condoning the controlling behavior of the one whom we seek to pacify. This raises an interesting and difficult question. Which is the more significant sin, to control others or to allow ourselves to be controlled?

I was once involved in a very difficult situation in Christian leadership. The congregation included a hurting lady who guarded her inner wounds with a powerful controlling mechanism of disapproval. Her whole countenance constantly expressed this disapproval towards most of the people in the church and how they went about their activities. We were all very intimidated by her and pathetically grateful if she uttered any encouraging comments. Her frowns and sighs at church meetings were amazingly effective in steering the course of the discussions. It was clear to everyone that her behavior was defiling relationships in the church, but confronting the issue just seemed too difficult.

I then experienced one of the few times that God has spoken to me in such a clear way. He asked me this question. "Why are you appeasing the controlling demon in this damaged lady?" I was shocked by the blunt reality of the situation. I had thought the sin was all hers, whereas God pointed out my sin of abdication. The fellowship was being directed more often by her controlling disapproval than by the voice of God. It was time to confront both her and the spiritual power that operated through her. It wasn't easy, but the eventual outcome was a dramatic new freedom for the whole church.

Fear of something or somewhere

Fear may relate to *someone* who has been controlling us but it can also be because of *something*. As a result of bad experiences in our lives we can find ourselves carrying powerful fears of things and places which, if left unresolved, can significantly control our lives. The original cause may have been due to someone's sin or carelessness, but the fear which remains is not directed towards a person but towards an object or place. These kinds of fear are called phobias. They are controlling fears which can be triggered today by circumstances similar to those which originally caused the problem.

The reason that we still carry the fear is that we were unable to find true safety and peace in the past, so we're left in the grip of the fear that overwhelmed us then. We deal with these fears usually by avoidance, but if this is stealing peace or driving us away from things which should be part of our daily lives, there's a problem of ungodly control. We may need to forgive others for originally putting us in fear, but we may also need to own the fact that we have given a place in our hearts for this fear to wrongly control our lives. Fear of failure, isolation, rejection, ridicule, trains, lifts, loud noises, water, hospitals, bats or illness; the list is endless.

Job understood the power of controlling fears when he said, *"For what I fear comes upon me, and what I dread befalls me"* (Job 3:25, NAS).

Thankfully we can come to God with these fears and be set free from the control which they have on our lives and the way that the enemy has used them against us

Control in church leadership

Those who stand at the front of a church have particular opportunity to either lead congregations into truth and freedom or to control them through deception, condemnation and criticism. It's an awesome responsibility to give direction to God's people. If there are unhealed places in the hearts of leaders they remain vulnerable to using 'soulish' methods in directing the people, even if this isn't done intentionally. Worship leaders can be wonderful musicians but may fall easily into using manipulative routines if their hearts are still struggling with unhealed insecurity. Teachers can be passionate about Kingdom truth but it can come with controlling condemnation if their hearts have not personally known the unconditional acceptance of their Heavenly Father. The hearers may respond to the message but they can be gripped more with the fear of punishment than with the limitless love of God.

The high pulpits of many traditional churches have, not without reason, often been described as being constructed to be several feet above contradiction. The job of the speaker is, with humility, to hold up a plumb-line of what God says is right and true. If the message comes with any sense of criticism or self righteousness, the hearers will experience control rather than true conviction, whether they realize it or not.

God hates control in a religious disguise. Our controlling prayer can use the words to try and direct those around us. Our controlling worship can demand a response through musical techniques. Our controlling preaching can demand a response through emotional and verbal techniques. No leader is going to be perfect, but if we remain open to God's correction and healing, He will have an increasingly clean vessel through whom to direct His people, without the defilement of control.

Aggressive control

In Christian groups, control often tends to be of the more subtle type, but even here dominating behavior is all too common, as it is in the world outside the church. In business, people are frequently trained to take advantage of the weakness in others and to exert authority by words, posture or gifts. In much business training, it's acceptable to clinch the deal by fair means or foul. Money, sex, holidays, parties, food, all hidden under the guise of corporate entertainment, are powerful weapons in the armory used for controlling business relationships.

Hostile, argumentative, critical and unsympathetic behavior is often applauded if it gets results. The end is seen to justify the means, so controlling your business client or your rivals is just part of the game. Courtesy, respect and good old-fashioned manners are seen as worthy attributes but not at the expense of losing the sale. Amazingly there are now many television programs, of a competitive nature, which revel in the humiliation of the losing participants. Maybe it's meant to add tension and excitement, but the underlying message is often that dominating your opponents is a praiseworthy goal. How different from the message which Jesus brings of the Kingdom of God!

Staying ahead of others

For many of us, we have become so used to how the world carries on in relationships that we're often completely oblivious of the subtle ways by which we also make sure that we don't lose our place in the crowd. Drawing attention to the weaknesses in others, questioning ability, reminding people of past mistakes and general gossip can all be used to control our position among our colleagues. Unchecked, it can grow into false accusation and feeding the bad reputation and insecurity of others, simply to maintain for ourselves a dominant position. Such controlling behavior can be masked under 'bringing things into the light', but the challenge is to very honestly look at our motives for such behavior. Is it intended to lift up Jesus or to lift up ourselves? It always seems easier to control from 'the moral high ground', where we can make judgments on others.

It can seem frightening for some leaders to think of losing their position and their control. Managers who feel threatened and fear that others will take their place may set up their staff for failure. Or they may try to make themselves indispensable, never fully sharing or delegating the jobs. Humiliation of others, disapproval and even over-protection can all be tools in the bag of those who feel they must control to survive. It happens in the work place, in families and unfortunately in churches. For many it becomes just a way of life, un-noticed and un-checked. This could be a good time to let God show us the truth of all our relationships.

Establishing a pecking order

My family kept chickens for many years. We housed four of them in a moveable chicken run and fed them on a combination of high protein feed and kitchen waste. We bought them at 'point of lay' from local suppliers from among hundreds of birds reared for egg-laying. It was very interesting to watch their behavior when first introduced to this new environment and to their newly selected colleagues. For about a week there would be constant pecking of each other until they had established the control regime in the chicken run. These were sometimes bloody contests but once settled it was clear that each knew exactly where she stood in the pecking order. Only occasional reminders were then needed to make sure no-one was stepping out of line!

Dare I suggest that a more subtle form of this can exist even in church groups? I'm not talking about the structure of godly authority that is essential for safety and effectiveness in the Body

of Christ, but the unseen control that seeks to establish a hierar-
chy of significance and power within the group. The disciples were
constantly challenged by how little Jesus followed the usual proto-
cols of the world. He brought a message that God's Kingdom was
about the seeking of a new heart not an improved status.

An argument broke out among the disciples as to which one of them
was the greatest. Jesus knew what they were thinking, so He took a
child, stood him by His side, and said to them, "Whoever welcomes
this child in My name, welcomes Me; and whoever welcomes Me,
also welcomes the One who sent Me. For the one who is least among
you all is the greatest."

Luke 9:46-48, GNB

Learning how to control

Linda was emotionally wounded as a small girl by an extremely
possessive mother and a very weak father. She had felt trapped and
powerless throughout her childhood. As a Christian, now in her
forties, she had begun to deal with her mother's stifling control,
even though she no longer lived with her parents. She started to
move into a new place of freedom after years of mental instability
when she forgave her mother and father and asked God to release
her from their destructive hold over her life.

But there was a problem in the healing process. Out of the deep
damage, rejection and isolation, she had developed powerful controlling techniques in her adult life in order to get the attention and
comfort she craved. The problem was that when she manipulated
others into responding to her needs, their attention never seemed
to meet the deep hunger for acceptance and love which was causing so much inner pain.

Her controlling techniques were unpleasant and numerous,
some learned from her mother and some through the painful experiences of adult life. She had violent tempers, sometimes damaging
both herself and the things around her. She threatened self-harm
and even suicide. She expressed her unhappiness at inappropriate

times with verbal outbursts, silences, a scowling face and abrasive comments towards those around her. She constantly displayed the identity of a victim or martyr amongst her colleagues at work, forcefully seeking their acknowledgment and comfort.

Of course we all realized that there was much pain mixed in with all her wrong behavior. The breakthrough came when she acknowledged that she could make a choice to stop trying to control the responses of those around her. This behavior had developed over many years and it took courage and determination to no longer be a victim demanding attention. She discovered that the more she put down her controls the more God was able to get through and bring real restoration and comfort to the hurting places. It was remarkable to see the gradual, but life-changing, freedom and wholeness that God brought.

Control by doing nothing

Amazingly we can control others as much by what we *don't* do as by what we *do*. Prisoners being interrogated are sometimes brought under the control of the interrogator by the withholding of food and water, only providing these when the prisoner's response is acceptable. People may not have withheld food from us but the control is just as powerful when love is withheld. Longing for a kind word or an approving comment can keep us continually 'on a string' to those with the ability and responsibility to hand these out. Of course this is particularly damaging between parents and children, but such control can be used by teachers, pastors, marriage partners and other relatives.

God designed us to need affirmation. It's one of the most important tasks of a father towards his son or daughter. Our Heavenly Father demonstrated clear affirmation to His Son Jesus.

> And the Holy Spirit came down upon Jesus in bodily form like a dove. And a voice came from heaven, "You are my own dear Son. I am pleased with you."
>
> Luke 3:22, GNB

Many children spent day after day of their childhood waiting for words like these from their earthly father. They desperately strived to please dad because the need to hear these words seemed to control their lives. There are many things that can be withheld from others. Depending on our position, we may be able to withhold affirmation, money, information, assistance or advice. The person who needs these things is held in a place of dependence on us, because we have the power to hold them back. The expression *'knowledge is power'* can be very true. Handing out little bits of information can give us a way to hold others under our control. Even the threat to resign from a position can be used to manipulate events to our favor. *"If I can't get my own way then I'm leaving"* is a very common threat used in the world and sometimes even in the church.

Money has always provided one of the most effective tools for getting our own way. If we have it and someone else doesn't, our ability to control them is as endless as our fund of money. From the beginning, men have bought the cooperation of others by giving money or possessions. Kings have controlled empires by giving gifts to the right people at the right time. Parents have kept their children in check by giving or withholding pocket money. Payment of money should be in response to what has been rightfully received in the way of labor or goods. It can be given as a free-will gift, of course, but in that case it should never have 'strings attached'. When we use it to win favor or to keep allegiance we have destroyed true relationship and merely purchased ungodly submission.

God designed human beings to enjoy a freedom of expression in relationships. Depending on the level of intimacy it's important to share time, thoughts and experiences with each other. It can be very controlling to never let others see how we really feel. The deepest place of sharing should be in the covenant of marriage, where we give ourselves in emotional and sexual intimacy. Unfortunately, this permits another powerful area of control when a marriage partner chooses not to talk, not to share their heart or give themselves in sexual union. It's certainly true that control can be just as effective through what we *don't do* as what we *do*.

Summary

The number of ways that we control is probably as numerous as the number of people who control. There are subtle ways and obvious ways, from emotional blackmail to threats of violence. We can exert force or withhold love. We learn from those around us and from experimenting with our own techniques. It can be conscious or unconscious behavior but either way it's sin when it's not using godly authority.

An almost universal element of control is fear. We tend to control the will of another person not so much by direct means but through their emotions, and particularly through the use of fear. People's choices are very powerfully motivated by intimidation.

We can control with the words that we speak or the words that we don't speak. We can control with the expression of our face or with our whole body language. We can control with the things we give to others and the things we withhold. It's time to look in the Bible at a well-known expert in the art of control. Her name was Jezebel.

Who is Jezebel?

A person or a spirit?

Jezebel was a historical figure whose story is comprehensively described in Kings 1 and 2. Indeed, her story revolves around a royal court immersed in rebellion against God and in destructive, controlling relationships with each other. Her story and her character are described in such detail that we find ourselves given an amazingly clear picture of the spiritual driving force behind her attitudes and behavior.

The controlling behavior of Jezebel is so intense and so clearly demonic that her name has become a useful label for this particular type of spiritual power. It seeks to rule in the world by operating through certain damaged individuals. Jesus pointedly picks up the name Jezebel to show the church of Thyatira exactly what enemy activity is operating in the congregation. He tells them that they have fallen into the trap of appeasing a powerful controlling spirit rather than walking in rightful godly authority.

> *But this is what I have against you: you tolerate that woman Jezebel, who calls herself a messenger of God. By her teaching she misleads my servants into practicing sexual immorality and eating food that has been offered to idols.*
>
> Revelation 2:20, GNB

As we read this passage in Revelation, we find that the demonic character described is remarkably similar to that operating in the character called Jezebel in the Old Testament. We are clearly dealing with the same spiritual power, which seeks to undermine godly order and authority and to find human vessels through which to promote disorder. Let's try to get the full picture of Jezebel.

Wrong spiritual covering opens a door for un-godly control

It was not enough for him (Ahab) to sin like King Jeroboam; he went further and married Jezebel, the daughter of King Ethbaal of Sidon, and worshiped Baal.

1 Kings 16:31, GNB

The spiritual covering and protection of God is established in our lives when we walk in His order and under His instructions. Families and nations know the blessing of God when individuals, and in particular the leaders, walk in godly obedience. Ahab was king over Israel, a significant position of authority and a vessel for God's protection and provision for the people. But, contrary to God's commands, he chose to marry outside of the children of Israel, to a Baal-worshipping woman called Jezebel. Indeed he actively rebels against God in erecting an altar to Baal in Samaria. Ahab had opened a dangerous door to the enemy, not just exposing his own family, but the whole nation.

Jezebel became the instrument of the enemy's control in the family but Ahab was certainly the one who invited this spiritual enemy into his house. Ungodly control always seeks to fill the spiritual vacuum created by the absence of right authority under God. Leaders are not just targets of undermining control; they are very often the door-openers, through personal sin and weakness.

Jezebel control will always seek to silence the true voice of God

And when Jezebel was killing the LORD's prophets, Obadiah took a hundred of them, hid them in caves in two groups of fifty, and provided them with food and water.

1 Kings 18:4, GNB

This spirit, which was working through Jezebel, will try to claim 'the moral high ground' by finding fault with others and accusing them. It promotes a strategy of division and is fully aware that the more people who can be brought 'on-side', the better will be the position of control. If others get trampled, so be it. The prophetic ministry is particularly vulnerable to this defiling power. This spirit hates godly anointing. One of the tactics of Jezebel is to try to become a dominant voice for imparting divine direction, albeit false. Often Jezebel will not directly usurp godly leadership, but will seek to influence and control leaders by apparently bringing God's revelation and wisdom.

It is here in the story of Jezebel that Elijah appears in order to declare the truth of godly authority and to make known the gross rebellion in this royal family. God hates the work of this powerful controlling spirit and He will not leave it hidden or unchallenged. Elijah comes with a different spirit, the Holy Spirit, a true anointing which brings godly prophecy and godly order. True prophesy brings such important empowering for God's people, but false prophesy is territory for the operation of the Jezebel spirit. God had given Elijah the unenviable task of exposing the enemy's lies so he met with King Ahab and called for a showdown.

"Now order all the people of Israel to meet me at Mount Carmel. Bring along the 450 prophets of Baal and the 400 prophets of the goddess Asherah who are supported by Queen Jezebel."

1 Kings 18:19, GNB

The result was absolute ridicule of the enemy's power and a supernatural defeat of those supporting this ambitious queen.

Elijah ordered, "Seize the prophets of Baal; don't let any of them get away!" The people seized them all, and Elijah led them down to Kishon Brook and killed them.

1 Kings18:40, GNB

But Jezebel remained alive and continued to provide the most important vessel for this destructive spirit to exercise control.

The Jezebel spirit is extremely intimidating

She [Jezebel] sent a message to Elijah: "May the gods strike me dead if by this time tomorrow I don't do the same thing to you that you did to the prophets." Elijah was afraid and fled for his life; he took his servant and went to Beersheba in Judah, leaving the servant there.

1 Kings 19:2-3, GNB

Remember that fear is a primary means of control. Threats can put us in fear and under the control of the one challenging us. We may be in fear of losing our good name, our status, our livelihood, our friends or even our life. Elijah felt the full force of this spiritual terrorism and buckled under its strength. This is a vicious spirit when given any license to undermine godly leadership.

The intimidation of Jezebel serves two purposes. One is to manipulate those who are in rightful authority to act in line with the enemy's plans and purposes. The second is to put the leader in fear of carrying out any confrontation of the ungodly control. I remember Bill talking about his very controlling wife whom he had loved dearly but whom he had constantly appeased for decades. "Anything for a quiet life," he would say. It may well have been quiet in the home but there was certainly no true peace, as long as Bill's fear allowed control of the family. One day Bill discovered the cost of ungodly appeasement when his son violently rebelled against his parents saying that he had had enough of the relentless domination of his mother and the frustrating apathy of his father.

Women may often be seen as the ones who most frequently *express* a Jezebel spirit of control but men are very often the ones who *appease* that spirit. Fear of Jezebel control gives authority to the spirit.

The Jezebel spirit can seem so helpful

How often have I heard that, "such and such a person may be causing offence in the fellowship through all the control, but at least they're getting the jobs done" One way of being able to assume an increasing control within a group is to appear indispensable. For tired leaders it can seem so very attractive when someone takes from us the burden of something for which we should have been personally responsible. But it's not right. If I'm the one who should be giving clear direction and I carelessly pass the responsibility to another, it can give an opportunity for this spirit to gain authority and power.

> *His [Ahab's] wife Jezebel went to him and asked, "Why are you so depressed? Why won't you eat?" He answered, "Because of what Naboth said to me. I offered to buy his vineyard or, if he preferred, to give him another one for it, but he told me that I couldn't have it!" "Well, are you the king or aren't you?" Jezebel replied. "Get out of bed, cheer up, and eat. I will get you Naboth's vineyard!"*
>
> 1 Kings 21:5-7, GNB

This spirit seeks out any weakness in godly order to obtain a foothold for influence, control and for further undermining of rightful authority. The apparent support by this spirit of those in leadership will be persuasive and deceptive. Secrecy will be an important tool to manipulate both people and situations. This spirit may offer an attractive end result, but it will always be through an ungodly process. Indeed there's no limit to the destructive capabilities of a Jezebel spirit operating within a weak authority structure and through a dysfunctional human vessel.

> *As soon as Jezebel received the message (that Naboth had been stoned), she said to Ahab, "Naboth is dead. Now go and take possession of the vineyard which he refused to sell to you."* . . . *There was no one else who had devoted himself so completely to doing wrong in the LORD's sight as Ahab, all at the urging of his wife Jezebel.*
>
> 1 Kings 21:15,25, GNB

The control in Jezebel was demonically inspired

We come, in this story of Queen Jezebel, to the time when God has decided to bring an end to the operation of this particular defiling spirit in the house of Ahab. Once sown into the family, the iniquity behind this spirit was set to bring destructive control down the generational line. It may seem extreme to us now but, under the Old Covenant, spiritual defilement was often eradicated by the destruction of the particular people who were promoting that spirit, in gross rebellion. On this occasion it was to be the removal of the whole of Ahab's family, not least his wife Jezebel. God is equally hostile to the work of this controlling spirit today, but by His grace, He has defeated the enemy through the death of Jesus, allowing us to be set free from the consequence of our rebellion.

God looks for those who will challenge the Jezebel spirit under His authority. The man chosen by God to deal with Ahab's household was Jehu. He set off to find Jezebel and was confronted by Ahab's son Joram, who suspected that Jehu was intending to destroy the family.

> *"Are you coming in peace?" Joram asked him. "How can there be peace," Jehu answered, "when we still have all the witchcraft and idolatry that your mother Jezebel started?"*
>
> 2 Kings 9:22, GNB

The peace that Joram was seeking was simply the *cover up* that expresses the deceptive character of the enemy, not the true peace which comes when sin is dealt with. Jehu was voicing the opinion of all those who had seen the iniquity in this royal family and, as a result, in the nation. Jezebel had been operating not just with ungodly controlling behavior, but by means of demonically empowered sorcery and witchcraft. The control from a Jezebel spirit is supernatural and works against the spiritual authority and the power of God.

It was clear to Jehu that this was God's time to completely destroy this power of darkness operating through Ahab's family. It wasn't long after this incident that both Joram and Jezebel were put to death, Jezebel being so utterly destroyed that there remained nothing of her to be either buried or commemorated.

> *When they reported this to Jehu, he said, "This is what the LORD said would happen, when he spoke through his servant Elijah: 'Dogs will eat Jezebel's body in the territory of Jezreel. Her remains will be scattered there like dung, so that no one will be able to identify them.'"*
>
> 2 Kings 9:36-37. GNB

Jezebel can be seductive especially when challenged

> *Jehu arrived in Jezreel. Jezebel, having heard what had happened, put on eye shadow, arranged her hair, and stood looking down at the street from a window in the palace.*
>
> 2 Kings 9:30, GNB

Sexuality and sex have always been used as devices for control. Men have been lured into situations, which they would never have submitted to, had it not been for the enticement of sexual favors. The Jezebel spirit is very familiar with the power of sexual attraction. We noted earlier that Jesus challenges the church at Thyatira with the way that they had permitted this characteristic manipulation by the enemy. They had been tolerating a deceptive and immoral spirit operating within the fellowship.

> *But this is what I have against you: you tolerate that woman Jezebel, who calls herself a messenger of God. By her teaching she misleads my servants into practicing sexual immorality and eating food that has been offered to idols.*
>
> Revelation 2:20, GNB

How often do we see leaders being drawn into sexual sin and finding themselves, their ministry and even their congregation destroyed? It can so often start with someone inappropriately 'supporting' a leader. Unchecked, this support may deepen from practical to emotional help and then finally turn into a sexual liaison.

A ruling spirit over Babylon

It's interesting to note that in chapter 47 of the book of Isaiah, the prophet sees very similar aspects of the enemy's character operating over the defiled city of Babylon. He describes the spiritual rule in the hearts of the people in ways that sound very much like the behavior which we have been seeing in Jezebel. Isaiah uses phrases, with regard to this spirit over the city, such as a *'proud queen'*, a *'sensual one'*, a *'woman of many sorceries and false prophecy'*, all sounding remarkably familiar.

It seems that this ruling spirit, with all the control characteristics of Jezebel, will look for opportunity to affect not just individuals but communities, cities and nations, drawing followers into both corporate and individual rebellion and promoting ungodly control. We would do well to look out for the character of this spirit in our communities and even our churches where sinful behavior in the past has given rights for the enemy to establish this type of defiled spiritual legacy. It was this ungodly inheritance in Ahab's family that determined God's radical cleansing of the royal family line.

The team at Ellel Ministries has come across many examples of churches battling today with a legacy of Jezebel control, because past issues have been left unresolved. Particular people may move on but the spirit can linger, gaining authority and power through the un-confessed sin of the past and the weaknesses or ignorance of those in current leadership.

We will look at this issue in more detail in the last chapter and see how God brings cleansing to churches as the leaders, in particular, bring these past and present sin issues into the light.

Jesus wants His church to be especially alert to the spirit of Jezebel

We see in the last part of chapter 2 of the book of Revelation, the church at Thyatira being torn apart by the conflict between the true authority of Christ and an idolatrous and immoral spirit, which is seducing the believers into false prophesy and false spirituality. The enemy's character being displayed here is *so* similar to that which was operating through Queen Jezebel. Deception, false religion, the undermining of leadership and seductive control are all here in this New Testament church.

The false teaching which is being promoted has apparently been fascinating many in the church, but Jesus makes it clear that this spirit, which is trying to get control, will eventually face certain destruction. He challenges the believers to stay true to Him and not to be destroyed along with those who have fallen under this deception.

> But the rest of you in Thyatira have not followed this evil teaching;
> you have not learned what the others call 'the deep secrets of Satan.'
> I say to you that I will not put any other burden on you. But until I
> come, you must hold firmly to what you have.
>
> Revelation 2:24-25, GNB

Summary

Jezebel was a historical figure who exhibited extreme control. Her name has been used to describe the characteristic nature of this demonically empowered type of control.

The character, which this spirit exhibits, is rebellious, arrogant, seductive, disapproving and destructive. This can lead to confused leadership, false anointing, sexual and emotional manipulation and false religious spirituality.

Jezebel's story within the royal family of King Ahab gives a very helpful insight into the workings of this controlling spiritual power, which looks for an absence of godly authority and order. Jesus reminds us, in His strong words to the church at Thyatira, that the Jezebel spirit is as active today as it was in the time of Ahab. We are to remain alert so that we neither appease this power of darkness not let it operate through us.

CHAPTER 7
Is Self-Control Good?

Who is ultimately in charge?

"He was amazingly self-controlled. Despite the terrible injustice towards his family, I never saw him get angry. We are all so proud of him."

Something is very wrong here. We were designed by God to be angry when there's injustice and to seek, with Him, a way to make things right. In fact we're told that this kind of self-control actually works in the enemy's favor, giving him a right to use the buried anger in a way that is destructive both to ourselves and to others.

> *Be angry and yet do not sin; do not let the sun go down on your anger, and do not give the devil an opportunity.*
> Ephesians 4:26-27, NAS

This passage tells us quite simply that even though we may think that we're in control of the suppressed angry feelings, ultimately it's the enemy who gets spiritual authority. Our emotional responses to the world around us were meant to be expressed at the time they were felt, not pushed into a dark corner. Jesus expressed joy, grief, loneliness and anger as His time on earth brought Him into contact with all the challenges of human life. His godly self-control led to rightful emotional responses which were without sin and always at one with His Father. His thoughts

and feelings were neither squashed down nor expressed explosively and He never gave the enemy an opportunity to have a place of control.

Controlling our emotions

So many phrases have been spoken over people's lives to encourage the wrongful control of emotions. Often it's part of the culture of the nation, the society or the family in which we were raised. A *'stiff upper lip'* is a classic characteristic of the British way of life but it can encourage a powerful suppression of distress, fear and pain. Inside we may be crying out for help but a choice is made to present a calm appearance, because we believe this to be all that's acceptable. It's actually ungodly self-control. How often do we hear parents saying to children, "don't cry, don't get upset or don't make a fuss." Of course children need to be encouraged to work towards a place of peace in any distressing situation, but that's very different from negating the God-given emotions which are meant to release the inner stress and help them reach out for empathy.

When a strong feeling occurs within us, there's usually a desire to express this by physical activity: speaking, crying, shouting, running, jumping, waving our hands about or stamping our feet. If we believe these to be unacceptable responses, we take control over our bodies and deny this important physical process. It's ungodly self-control. Of course this isn't to say that ranting, raving and emotional tantrums are necessary in each situation of emotional distress. When the Spirit of God is given control, our responses can be appropriate and effective in bringing real release and resolution to the situation.

The mechanics of ungodly self-control

We are amazingly complex creatures. We have a physical body working in conjunction with our human spirit, by means of the choices made in our human soul. Ideally the Holy Spirit directs our lives moment by moment, giving God's wisdom for all the situations which we experience through the day. Our soul is picking up the physical, emotional and spiritual sensations around us and making choices to direct the body, hopefully in line with what God says is right.

The problem is that the still small voice of God can get drowned out by strong voices of disapproval, discouragement and intimidation in the world around us. Instead of walking according the Spirit of God we frequently walk according to our human nature. The soul rises up (with 'soulish' behavior) and takes control, denying spiritual truth and following the direction of the deceptive ruler of this world. Through fear of rejection, fear of failure, fear of disapproval or embarrassment, we move unconsciously into ungodly self-control.

Messages are sent around the body directing ourselves to, "take a deep breath, swallow hard, don't show how you feel, disconnect with the feelings inside, put on a brave face, don't let others see that you are upset, don't make it worse by crying, leave it all behind, move on." The trouble is that the feelings don't just go away but remain unexpressed and trapped inside us in the place of control. The enemy can rule over this place. Perishable food shut away in a cupboard, and foolishly ignored, may be out of sight but sooner or later the whole house becomes polluted by the wrong decision which was made.

Those who live as their human nature tells them to, have their minds controlled by what human nature wants. Those who live as the Spirit tells them to, have their minds controlled by what the Spirit wants. To be controlled by human nature results in death; to be controlled by the Spirit results in life and peace.

Romans 8:5-6, GNB

The body needs to be under right spiritual control

Without the right boundaries we are very vulnerable to emotional and spiritual damage. Under the Lordship of Jesus, our human spirit rests in safety and well-being. 'Soulish' behavior leaves our spirit unguarded and open to the enemy's infiltration. All rightful spiritual authority flows down from the Spirit of God, into the spirit, the soul and the body of man. When this flow is interrupted by ungodly self-control, we're like an unguarded city.

> *Like a city that is broken into and without walls is a man who has*
> *no control over his spirit.*
>
> Proverbs 25:28, NAS

When our whole being is *under* right authority it's *in* right authority. Under the authority of Jesus we are governed and indwelt by the Holy Spirit. We are then operating in godly self-control, a fruit of the Spirit (Galatians 5:23). The body is free to act in every way as God intended but within His covenant commands which bring spiritual safety and the fulfillment of destiny. When someone is out of this rightful control and operating in sinful behavior, all peace is lost and it becomes very destructive both to the person and to those around. This is the fruit of 'soulishness', which is control by our human nature.

> *For what our human nature wants is opposed to what the Spirit*
> *wants, and what the Spirit wants is opposed to what our human*
> *nature wants. These two are enemies, and this means that you can-*
> *not do what you want to do.*
>
> Galatians 5:17, GNB

Controlling our mind

Ungodly self-control is not just about shutting down the emotions. There are many techniques, which have long been taught, for control of the mind. When these techniques over-ride the rule of the Holy Spirit, we're in danger of handing over control to the enemy. Many forms of meditation, for example the techniques of yoga, encourage us to empty our minds using physical and verbal exercises to control the body. We're then open to whatever mystical forces may be wishing to enter our thinking and to direct our will.

In contrast, the Word of God encourages us to seek the *renewing* of our minds, not by any control techniques but by simply offering ourselves to God to be convicted of sin and to know His amazing cleansing.

> *So then, my friends, because of God's great mercy to us I appeal to you: offer yourselves as a living sacrifice to God, dedicated to his service and pleasing to him. This is the true worship that you should offer. Do not conform yourselves to the standards of this world, but let God transform you inwardly by a complete change of your mind. Then you will be able to know the will of God, what is good and is pleasing to him and is perfect.*
>
> Romans 12:1-2, GNB

Positive thinking techniques can seem very attractive to those struggling with discouragement and low self-esteem. Although the Bible (in Philippians 4:8) encourages us to dwell on those things that are true and right and pure, it does *not* instruct us to deny the reality of sin and pain. When we strive to take control of what's happening in our minds rather than surrendering our thoughts to the Spirit of God, we risk releasing control to the powers of darkness.

With certain alternative therapies we can unwittingly enter into techniques of self hypnosis, bringing our minds into a place of controlled dissociation. God designed our body, soul and spirit to operate in unity; the enemy thrives on division. The mind is precious and critical territory within our being, which needs to be carefully guarded and nurtured under the safe control of our Heavenly Father.

Controlling our identity

We live in a world where image seems to be everything. Life will *be* OK, we believe, if we *look* OK. But who decides on what image is acceptable? We are made in the image of God, and it's good for us to make the best of what He has created. Our identity is established by God in our human spirit and demonstrated in the whole of our being. However, through wounding, insecurity and rejection, if we strive to move away from the person that God created us to be, then we have taken wrongful control of our own image and identity. We actually begin to live a lie; unreality is enemy territory.

The first chapter of the Bible tells us that animals were created to bear the image of one another (*made after their kind*), unlike human beings who were created to bear the image of their Creator (*according to Our likeness*). If we seek to make ourselves acceptable by giving ourselves an image which the world tells us is right, we deny our unique God-given identity. We have actually taken control over our human spirit, rejecting the place of our true identity.

Our sexuality is a significant part of that identity under God. There can be huge damage in this area through abuse and neglect in our early lives, but the wounding is not healed by denying our God-given masculinity or femininity. Many women, who have been sexually abused in childhood, find it very difficult to present a wholly feminine identity. It seems too vulnerable. Many men, unaffirmed by dad in their sexual identity, find it difficult to embrace a fully masculine image. When we take wrongful control over the expression of our sexuality we give spiritual rights to the enemy and allow him to promote disorder and disorientation.

Controlling the functions of our physical body

Eating is a fundamental aspect of human life. It's meant to be not just an *essential* activity but a *pleasurable* one. God intended that meal times should be enjoyable both individually and corporately. Eating together with family and friends builds relationship. Unfortunately it's also a powerful opportunity for ungodly control. Good experiences with food should be associated with acceptance, freedom, comfort and well-being; bad experiences can result in just the opposite.

Some people have a remembrance of meals as small children being times of distressing family dysfunction and strong parental control. It's not unusual for meals to be presented by mothers in such a way that to refuse any part of it is seen as rejecting a person. Fathers can easily just add to the sense of tension the table, as they join in the pressure to eat in particular ways or certain quantities.

Young children seem to learn very early that not eating in the way that mum or dad seem to require, provides a way of expressing their inner feelings and taking a measure of control over their lives. As we grow up, eating obviously affects our physical bodies. If, for example through abuse, we have a dislike of our bodies, then too much or too little food can be a way of taking control over our appearance. At the same time there will be a controlling effect on those around us as they seek to normalize our eating behaviors. We quickly learn that food can be a powerful tool in our desire to take some control, even as a form of rebellion, especially if our childhood eating experiences were times of tension.

We can change the look of our bodies, not just by food intake, but also through exercise, weight training, body building and even martial arts. There's nothing wrong with good exercise, but if there's an obsessive desire to control our body shape and our ability through such activities, we can find that we're losing control to the enemy's power. Particular methods of exercise may be based on foundational principles which could be spiritually harmful. We need to be wise in discerning what could be potentially unsafe.

A man called Joseph Pilates, who was born in 1880 and studied yoga and Zen meditation, developed an exercise regime which he called 'Contrology'. In 1945 he wrote, *'Contrology is complete coordination of body, mind and spirit. Through Contrology, you first purposefully acquire complete control of your body and then through proper repetition of its exercises you gradually and progressively acquire that natural rhythm and coordination associated with all your subconscious activities.'*

This method of exercise is now called *Pilates* and has become very popular, including among Christians. It is worth taking a moment to ask ourselves whether such a form of exercise, bearing in mind the roots, is actually putting the body under ungodly control, especially when the techniques claim to bring spiritual restoration.

ɔntrol, the more
away

hristian young man called Mike, who spent hours at the gym every day build- learning karate. He had a history of low ιing had made him feel good. He came for ιegun to realize that the more his body was developing in strengtι and ability, the more aggressive his behaviour was becoming. He was alarmed that the aggression sometimes burst out against his wife and friends.

Most martial arts are based on ancient beliefs that particular techniques of body and mind control will invite spiritual empowerment. This power was seen to come through the manipulation of a universal life force called *'Ch'i* (in Chinese) or *'Ki'* (in Japanese). In fact the names of some of the martial arts such as Aikido (meaning *the way of spiritual harmony*) demonstrate the belief behind this defensive technique. It was not without reason that Jesus declared so clearly that He is *'the Way and the Truth and the Life'* (John 14:6). If we look for spiritual harmony in our body by following any other way than through Jesus, we risk giving the enemy control. It can be an open invitation to the demonic realm.

Realizing that there was something very wrong about his obsessive visits to the gym, Mike brought the issue before the Lord in confession and he was wonderful set free from the aggressive spirit which had been given rights to control a part of his life. Sometimes when we think that we're taking control of our lives to improve ourselves, we can be unwittingly handing over that same control to the powers of darkness. Our bodies are vessels for spiritual authority in this world. We can be used for the good purposes of God or the destructive purposes of the enemy. We are the ones able to give control of our lives to whom we please. Animals don't have a choice about who puts a controlling yoke on their backs. We *do* have a choice and the best choice is Jesus.

Take my yoke and put it on you, and learn from me, because I am gentle and humble in spirit; and you will find rest. For the yoke I will give you is easy, and the load I will put on you is light.

Matthew 11:29-30, GNB

How interesting that one meaning of the word *yoga* is *yoke*.

Controlling our 'bad side'

Christians have a problem. As followers of Jesus we hopefully seek to reflect His character. He was and is perfect, and we would like to be exhibiting a lot more of His goodness and a lot less of our old sinfulness. There are two ways of seeking to achieve this, but only one of them works. God's way is that we let the Holy Spirit take control and He convicts us of the sinful areas in our lives. We then confess, repent and let Him empower a change of heart. The other way is that *we* take control and do our best to hide away the parts of our lives that we consider weak, painful or unacceptable. It doesn't work because we are simply putting part of our lives into darkness and under enemy control.

Much as we would like it to be effective, dissociation from our sinful nature doesn't bring holiness. We must acknowledge and confess our sinful human nature and then starve it into ineffectiveness by walking in daily submission to the Spirit of God. Dissociation from any part of ourselves is ungodly self-control, but it's surprisingly common.

Many of us were encouraged as little children to be a *good boy* or a *good girl*, but without being given God's way of achieving it. Hiding the *bad boy* or the *bad girl* may have seemed the only option and it may still be our unconscious plan for becoming more like Jesus. We used to have a small poster in our kitchen at home which said '*Let go and let God*'. In other words, the sanctification process in our lives will never be by our control, if that has replaced God's control.

Handing over control

The body has many needs of care and nurture. These needs intensify and go out of balance when we have been wounded. Trying to meet these needs can become overwhelming and lead to sinful choices in seeking some solution to the anxieties within. We will not be looking in depth, in this book, at addictive or obsessive behaviors, but it's important to realize that the word *addiction* literally means to give up (or hand over) part of our lives to something. It's a choice to give away control of part of ourselves to a substance or to a pattern of behavior.

There are countless reasons why people walk into addictive behavior, but the foundational issue is one of distress in the human heart. We look for significance, comfort, acceptance or escape, and a certain substance or activity seems to meet the need. Unfortunately we are, in effect, handing over control, for meeting that particular need, to something that's not God's way. Not only can this give opportunity for chemical and emotional dependency but it can give the enemy spiritual authority over a part of our lives.

When we choose to wrongly give away control of any part of our being, for whatever reason, the powers of darkness are only too willing to take hold of this ground. Whether the activities or substances are legal or illegal, nothing should be used to meet our needs in opposition to the One who desires to provide for us all protection and provision. To be truly at peace we can only serve one master. Paul puts it very clearly.

> *Someone will say, "I am allowed to do anything." Yes; but not everything is good for you. I could say that I am allowed to do anything, but I am not going to let anything make me its slave.*
>
> 1 Corinthians 6:12, GNB

Where can we go for help?

When we see that certain issues have got a wrong control in our lives, many of us will look for help from anyone who might offer a solution. There are huge numbers of people and organizations offering therapy. From mainstream medical practitioners to alternative therapists, the options are endless, but we need discernment. Many in the medical profession seem to understand that people are more than just physical beings and there's much talk these days of *holistic* treatment. This generally means that the therapy seeks to bring order to body, mind (soul) *and* spirit. But herein lies the problem.

As soon as the treatment has a spiritual aspect, we need to be very sure that the spiritual restoration is in safe hands. I strongly suggest that Jesus Christ has the only *truly* safe hands to deal with the deep needs of the human spirit. Only He can come with the true freedom of God's Kingdom.

> *Happy are those who know they are spiritually poor; the Kingdom of heaven belongs to them!*
>
> Matthew 5:3, GNB

Hundreds of therapies now available in the 'West' originate from ancient beliefs in the need to restore a balanced flow of the (*Chi* or *Ki*) universal spirit through the human body. This is not the Holy Spirit! For example Reiki (meaning Universal Life Force Energy) is an occult therapy which, though claiming to bring harmony to the body, is far more likely to bring demonic control. We need to be very careful, especially as Christians, as to *where*, and *to whom*, we go for help. We always need to ask the question, "Who's in control here?"

Susan came for prayer one day and told us the story of how she went to a hypnotherapist for help with an eating addiction. She remembered that the eating disorder seemed to disappear but an alcohol addiction started only a few months later. We explained to Susan that under hypnosis she had chosen to give control of part of her mind to the therapist, however well-meaning the person was. She was convicted by the Lord that this hadn't been His way for her restoration. As we prayed she experienced a powerful release from the demonic control and false healing which had become established during the treatment sessions. Susan was at last able to seek the Lord for true freedom from both the addictions and the roots of wounding which had led to the disorders.

Summary

Under the direction of the Holy Spirit, we can increasingly demonstrate the fruit of godly self-control. As we respond to God's conviction of the sinful areas of our lives, we can be empowered by Him to exercise rightful restraint and so walk less and less under the direction of our sinful nature.

> *But the Spirit produces love, joy, peace, patience, kindness, good-ness, faithfulness, humility, and self-control. There is no law against such things as these.*
>
> Galatians 5:22-23, GNB

Ungodly self-control occurs when we reject the overall author-ity of Jesus, deny the voice of the Spirit, and decide that *we know best*. It can be exercised over our emotions, our mind, our physical bodies and even over any part of our lives which we consider unac-ceptable. Such control is frequently the consequence of rejection and abuse from others.

We inflict control upon ourselves in an attempt to minimize pain and maximize our significance or acceptance with those around us. The problem is that it doesn't work and only leads to our being controlled by our sinful behaviors, which can then be empowered by the demonic realm.

It's time to consider how relevant all this might be to each of us.

CHAPTER 8

Is Control a Problem for Me?

Getting personal

At the beginning of this book I posed a question that I believe should be asked by every Christian: "Day by day, who or what controls my life?" We would like to answer that by saying, "Jesus is Lord of all I believe, all I do and all I say." However, unresolved fears, the wrongful hold of some relationships, and even our own 'soulish' self-control all inevitably battle against the goal of Jesus being our only master. For some people it's only too obvious that control has significantly affected them. For many of us, however, we have got so used to the way we conduct our lives, that we may be unconscious of how we're being controlled or how we exercise control over others.

Because of our sinful nature, ungodly control of people, control of situations and even control over our own lives becomes a natural response to the way that this world has hurt us. Unfortunately, being unaware of the extent of control operating around us doesn't protect us from the harm that it does.

Ungodly control in our lives causes damage to ourselves and to others. We need the revelation and conviction of God to be able to see what's happening in us and around us. Then we have the opportunity to let God bring freedom and restoration as we allow His Spirit to increasingly govern every aspect of our being.

A simple challenge

The rest of this chapter contains lists of questions. The purpose is to prompt us to think a little more deeply about this issue of control and give God an opportunity to bring light into places of darkness. *Yes* answers to the questions are an indication that ungodly control could be an issue for us. This isn't supposed to be a perfect or detailed analysis of the issue, but simply a starting place for seeking the heart and the voice of God.

If you decide to answer the questions, go through them fairly quickly not trying to evaluate them too deeply. Don't fall into condemnation if you find many of your answers are *yes*, but let God bring conviction that will draw you to a place of response. The next chapter contains suggestions for how you can bring these issues of control before God. Remember that *'if the Son sets you free, then you will be really free'* (John 8:36, GNB). He so wants our freedom.

Am I being, or have I been, wrongly controlled by someone ?

The questions relate to a current relationship but they're just as relevant to a relationship which may be unresolved from the past.

Yes answers may indicate that I am being wrongly controlled by *someone*.

- Do I harbor a fear concerning a particular person?
- Do my own feelings and opinions seem to be dismissed by them?
- Do I have to be particularly careful of upsetting this person?
- Am I indecisive when around this person?
- Do I take steps to avoid this person if it is possible?
- Do I feel unsafe with this person?
- Does the person make me feel angry?
- Am I more likely than usual to get things wrong in response to this person?
- Do I feel particularly grateful when this person is kind or approving towards me?

- Am I particularly dependent on advice or treatment from this person?
- Does this person make me feel guilty or ashamed?
- Does this person seem to dismiss my abilities?
- Am I unable to have heart-felt fellowship with this person?

Am I being wrongly controlled by something?

We learn to avoid things which we don't like but sometimes the avoidance has become so strong that our lives can be seriously controlled by the fears. Also, in looking for significance or comfort for inner distress, we can let certain routines and substances (such as alcohol) control our lives.

Yes answers may indicate that I am being wrongly controlled by *something*.

- Do I avoid certain types of places?
- Do I avoid certain types of people?
- Do I avoid certain types of travel?
- Do I do certain things in secret?
- Are alcoholic drinks, cigarettes, cups of coffee etc. essential aspects of my daily / weekly routine?
- Are certain TV programs or Internet sites a 'must'?
- Do I get distressed if my routine is disrupted?
- Do I experience panicky feelings in certain circumstances?
- Am I particularly dependent on a certain therapy?
- Do I avoid activities in which I might fail?
- Do I avoid activities that put me in front of people?
- Do I find it hard to join in with others?
- Do I get particularly anxious before certain occasions?
- Do I feel most at ease when I have found a way of escaping?

Do I control other people?

Remember that we can get so used to doing this that it has just become an unconscious way of life. We may be the last one to see the problem!

Yes answers may indicate that I am controlling *others*.

- Do people seem to avoid real relationship with me?
- Do my relationships with others often break down?
- Do I dislike working under someone's direction?
- Do I tend to do my own thing?
- Do I prefer not to be dependent for my needs on other people?
- Do I find it difficult to receive help, gifts or advice from others?
- Am I fearful when not in control of the situation?
- Do others see me as difficult or critical?
- Do I have to remind people of my authority?
- Do I tend to ignore other people's opinions?
- Is there un-forgiveness or judgment in my heart towards others?
- Do I avoid delegating to others?
- Do I constantly check up on those to whom I *have* delegated responsibility?

Do I wrongly control myself?

Am I stopping myself being free to be *me*? There is a godly self-control, which is the fruit of Holy Spirit authority in our lives, but many of us have failed to see that we have taken charge, without Him.

Yes answers may indicate that *I'm* controlling the person whom God made me to be.

- Do I find it difficult to express how I really feel?
- Is it a long time since I cried, laughed or showed anger in an appropriate way?
- Do I hate being caught unprepared?
- Does my diet, exercise or routine often take precedence over my relationships?
- Is my way of being right with God generally through what I achieve?

- Do people ever say – I don't really *know* you?
- Do I sometimes think I don't really *know* myself?
- Is maintaining appearance more important than true relationship?
- Do I tend towards perfectionism?
- Do I shut away what I don't like about myself?
- Am I still feeling guilty for past mistakes?
- Is what I say sometimes different from what's in my heart?
- Is my way of behaving with other people something of a pretence?

Summary

Sometimes the hardest part of being restored by God is recognizing the real need. This chapter has offered an opportunity to explore the issue of ungodly control in our lives. Sometimes we do need to ask ourselves difficult questions. Jesus often did that with those people who came to Him.

The answers to these questions may result in a strong indication that something needs to be sorted out. What's far more important than *yes* or *no* answers to searching questions is the conviction of God that it's time to bring something before Him in truth.

He brings conviction only for the purpose of helping us into freedom and healing. We shall now look at the steps which we can take to deal with wrongful control in our lives.

CHAPTER 9

Finding Freedom

Peter the disciple – an experienced controller

What encouragements there are in the many Bible accounts of the disciple Peter! We find that he's so like us and that he had so much to learn about truly being a *follower* of Jesus. Because of all his life experiences and insecurities, Peter thought that he could and should always take control, even with Jesus. From building unnecessary tents on a mountain to cutting off people's ears, Peter constantly felt it necessary to take charge of the situation. It seems crazy to us now as we read about Peter's behaviors.

The problem was that he had clearly been so used to taking command in every situation, he just went on doing what he believed that he did best. That was sorting out everything and everybody. He had just the same problem with his sinful human nature as we do, and he also found himself giving the enemy just the same opportunities that we can do, if we assume wrongful control. Peter even tried to take charge of the destiny of Jesus.

> *From that time on, Jesus began to say plainly to his disciples, "I must go to Jerusalem and suffer much from the elders, the chief priests, and the teachers of the Law. I will be put to death, but three days later I will be raised to life." Peter took him aside and began to rebuke him. "God forbid it, Lord!" he said. "That must never happen to you!" Jesus turned around and said to Peter, "Get away from me,*

Satan! You are an obstacle in my way, because these thoughts of
yours don't come from God, but from human nature."

Matthew 16:21-23, GNB

It was a direct challenge to Peter to give up trying to control his own life and that of everyone else. In a wonderful way Jesus saw through the sinful behavior into a heart that was willing to change. Peter was given the opportunity one morning, on a beach beside the Sea of Galilee, to decide who was going to be in control of his future. It was a tough challenge, but he decided that it would always be Jesus, the One whom he had come to love above all others (John 21:15-17). Jesus then told him that this decision would eventually result in his giving up his life in the service of his Master.

I am telling you the truth: when you were young, you used to get
ready and go anywhere you wanted to; but when you are old, you
will stretch out your hands and someone else will tie you up and
take you where you don't want to go.

John 21:18, GNB

Who controls your life and mine? It's at the heart of the spiritual battle which rages in and around all human beings, whether they realize it or not. There's a rightful spiritual authority which comes from Jesus Christ and which God desires should operate *over* each one of us and *through* each one of us. There's also a spiritual world-ruler, called Satan, who seeks to usurp that authority by using our sinfulness. Amazingly, the choice of who has the ultimate control in our lives rests with ourselves.

Dealing with wrong control definitely agrees with God

We need have no doubt that God delights in bringing freedom from the effects of control. We can bring before Him the sin of others who have controlled us but we shouldn't be surprised if He also shows us that we too have used control as a means of trying to deal with our hurting heart. God's people have, it seems, always been keen to perform religious activity but have rarely been willing to address to real sin issues. Through Isaiah, God spells out those things which are really important to Him. Significant among these is His hatred of oppressive control.

> *When you fast, you make yourselves suffer; you bow your heads low like a blade of grass and spread out sackcloth and ashes to lie on. Is that what you call fasting? Do you think I will be pleased with that?*
>
> *The kind of fasting I want is this: Remove the chains of oppression and the yoke of injustice, and let the oppressed go free.*
>
> Isaiah 58:5-6, GNB

If others have controlled us, we can choose to forgive them and break free from the legacy of bondage. If we've been the one controlling, we can confess, repent and enter into a new lifestyle of freedom. Let's look at some steps that we can take to break free from all aspects of control. Each step below includes a suggestion for how we can bring the situation before the Lord and find His freedom. All of these steps, especially the deliverance from the powers of darkness (step 6), are best done alongside one or two Christian brothers or sisters, who understand the issues and are willing to stand in agreement with us.

Step 1. If we say we have no sin... .

No doubt we have *all* been wounded by the sin of others but it's very often important to start with our own sin. None of us has led a life without using ungodly control at some time against those around us. Let God bring conviction as you take time to think about relationships, past and present, at home, at work and in the church. When and how have you striven to get the upper hand in relationships, demanding recognition of your position in the group, rather than being willing to wash the feet of your brothers and sisters?

Many have been given a place of godly authority but have missed the straight line, through abdication on the one hand or ungodly control on the other. Many of us have been frustrated by the spiritual disorder in the family, the workplace or in church and we have sought to direct others with our manipulative skills, believing that the good end result will surely justify the doubtful means. This will never be so in God's Kingdom. For many of us, coming from a wounded past, we just want to experience less pain in relationships, and the use of control has seemed to be part of the answer.

There *is* a radically different way of behaving. This way is to walk *under* and to walk *in* godly authority and to stop condoning wrong control.

A suggestion for what to say:

Father God, I see that Jesus has all authority in heaven and on earth but He has never exercised wrong control. I confess that I have allowed ungodly control to operate through me and against others, contrary to Your will for my life. I also acknowledge patterns of control in my parents and forebears. I choose to renounce my sinful behaviors and not to give any further opportunity for this legacy of wrong control.

Father, thank You for forgiving me and cleansing me, in Jesus name.

Step 2. Have I allowed people and things to control me?

There is one more thing we should do before dealing with those who have sinned against us. It's important to acknowledge that, for many reasons and not least fear, we have sometimes appeased, rather than confronted, those who have controlled us. As little children we probably didn't have a choice about who controlled us, but as adults we may often have followed a path of appeasement rather than challenge, in order to avoid the discomfort of trying to establish godly order.

Jesus challenged those who wrongly tried to control Him. He refused to let the religious opposition get their way until the moment when He knew the Father was telling Him give up His life. His death was the result of His choice to be obedient, not a result of the enemy's desire to control.

It's not just people who have controlled us. Through the traumas of life, fear can get a hold and leave us gripped by many different phobias, often irrational, but powerful none-the-less. What have we avoided doing in order not to have to face our areas of fear? Jesus says many times to His disciples '*do not fear*'. Unresolved fears can mean that our choices are made all too often because of fears, rather than because of the voice of God.

What activities, therapies or substances (such as nicotine) have we given control to, in order to try to meet the places of need inside? In trying to find acceptance, healing, comfort or escape, what have we allowed to get a hold over our lives? Whether it's work, exercise, alcohol, smoking, television, the Internet or some unhelpful therapy, it's time to choose to follow just one master.

A suggestion for what to say:

Father God, I confess that I have sinned by letting people and things control my life, rather than following You in all that I do, and trusting You in all that I need. I confess that I have sometimes taken what seemed to be the easy route of appeasing difficult people, rather than taking the godly route of confronting those who have controlled me.

I choose not to let fear of people, things or situations, including . . . (name who/what God has shown you) rule my life. In seeking to meet my needs, I choose not to give wrong control of any part of my life to substances, activities or therapies, including . . . (name those things that God has shown).

I receive Your forgiveness and cleansing in Jesus name.

Step 3. Who has had a wrongful control over my life?

Let's take a moment to consider the journey of life which we have walked up to this day. When has godly authority over our lives given way to ungodly control from a parent, a teacher, a leader, an employer, a spouse, a pastor, a therapist, a friend or a relative? Does a little fear still linger when we think of this person? Do we recognize now that some of the enemy's power was operating through them and onto us?

We can't change what happened nor can we necessarily change the person who has controlled us, but we *can* walk free from the ungodly yoke which was placed upon us, by choosing to forgive them. The control may have been overt domination or subtle manipulation. Either way it was sin. It does not dishonor parents or anyone else to acknowledge their sinfulness in the area of control.

Forgiveness should never belittle the offence nor should it look for excuses for the offender. Forgiveness faces the issue of sin head on but allows us to make a decision to release people who are in debt to us because of their sin against us.

A suggestion for what to say:

Father God, I acknowledge that godly authority will not harm me and I choose not to be in fear of those who are operating in godly order. However, I recognize that . . . (say the person's name) has had a wrong controlling influence over me by . . . (Speak out the details of how they controlled) and this has taken a grip on my life. I choose now, by an act of my free will, to forgive them for their words and actions and to release them into the freedom of my forgiveness, in Jesus name.

Step 4. Removing the yoke

When we have experienced the control of someone in our lives, we can get tied to them in a way that remains unseen and unresolved until we seek God's freedom. The yoke of authority from Jesus over believers does no harm, but a harsh yoke of ungodly control can hold us in damaging bondage. It needs removal. Paul gives the example of a controlling relationship where there is an unbelieving partner. He encourages us to avoid getting into such relationships.

> *Be ye not unequally yoked together with unbelievers: for what fellowship hath righteousness with unrighteousness? And what communion hath light with darkness?*
>
> 2 Corinthians 6:14, KJV

Avoidance may be too late for us in this particular relationship but freedom is always an option. We may now recognize that our thinking, our emotions and our choices have all been affected by the wrong control of another person. In other words our soul has been tied to them in the spiritual darkness and oppression of the relationship.

We forgave them in the last step but now it's time to break free from the unseen grip which the relationship may still be having on us. Sometimes we need to stop for a moment and check that there's nothing which might hold us spiritually tied to their control. Items may need returning or destroying where there are unresolved issues connected with written agreements, money, gifts, letters, photos and the like.

A suggestion for what to say:

Father God, I have fully released . . . (say their name) into my forgiveness. I now choose to walk free from the hold which this relationship has had over me, through their words and their behavior towards me.

I claim freedom from the ungodly soul-tie with . . . (Repeat their name) which has been a controlling bondage in my life. I ask Lord that there will be a complete separation of my own true identity from that of . . . (Repeat their name), and that I can be restored into the uniqueness and wholeness of the person that You created me to be.

I declare the ungodly yoke broken in the precious name of Jesus.

Step 5. Those who have controlled my life . . . does that include me?

It's time to consider how I have controlled myself. We have seen that Holy Spirit-directed self-control is a good fruit in our lives, but self-control governed by our sinful human nature develops rotten fruit. To try and make sense of this rejecting, image-centered, disapproving world, most of us have learned to control something of our emotions, our thinking, our image, our body or how we present ourselves to those around us in the home, the workplace and the church.

The key controller within us is the will of our sinful soul, which takes charge, ignores God's truth and crushes the true identity which God planted in our human spirit. We have an opportunity today to seek restoration to the amazing, unique, God-created and whole person who was made in our Creator's image. We truly need to *'let go and let God'*.

A suggestion for what to say:

Father God, I want to discover the true meaning of godly self-control. I renounce the fear of feeling out of control and I choose to let the Holy Spirit direct me and grow good fruit in my life. I confess that in many ways such as . . . (try to name a few), I have taken wrongful control over my emotions, my mind, my body, my creativity, my identity and even my destiny in You.

I renounce sinful self-pronouncements and ungodly coping mechanisms, which I thought would protect me. I confess that I have shut off from the parts of myself which I dislike, trying to present only an acceptable image. I recognize Lord that only You can change my heart and make me more like You.

Thank you that I am forgiven and I can be cleansed from all unrighteousness, in the name of Jesus.

Step 6. Deliverance issues

Once control has been handed back to Jesus and we have received God's forgiveness, all authority or rights, which the powers of darkness had opportunity to use against us, are removed. This changes the situation from spiritual darkness to light. Demons cannot sustain their activity in the light and can be expelled under the authority of Jesus.

Whether we have exercised control over others or we have suffered the abuse of controlling authority over our lives, the prayers which we have spoken out in the steps above, clear the way for cleansing from the enemy's spiritual defilement. Bearing in mind that we live in families, communities and nations which have opened the door to a powerful spiritual rule of control, it can be useful to bind that spiritual rule under the authority of Jesus as we seek freedom for our own personal lives.

The same ruling spirit which operated through Ahab's household, in his wife Jezebel and in the church at Thyatira is still very active today. We will look at this issue in the church in a little more in the last chapter. In the meantime we simply need to recognize the reality of a corporate spiritual defilement which exists, because of unresolved sin, over groups of people and over the land or buildings which they occupy.

A suggestion for what to say:

I acknowledge the ruling spirit of Jezebel control which has been given rights in my family, church and community through sin. I address you in the name of Jesus and hold you bound to His authority as I seek personal freedom from the spirits of control in my own life.

I address now the unclean spirits, which have had a foothold in my life through ungodly control both over me and through me. Under the authority of Jesus I drive out spirits of . . . (let the Lord show you the demonic controlling powers which have been operating, such as domination, rebellion, witchcraft, Jezebel, fear, infirmity, independence and false healing).

I command these spirits to leave every part of my body.

Step 7. Release from control and healing for the whole of the body

In Luke chapter 13, there's an amazing account of Jesus restoring a woman who had been bent over double for eighteen years. He releases her from the spiritual bondage and then lays hands on her to bring physical healing into her body. When a damaging spiritual yoke has been bearing down on us through ungodly control, it's only to be expected that our emotional and physical bodies will have suffered significant damage.

In the same passage, Jesus describes this two-stage restoration (the spiritual and then the physical) as being similar to untying and releasing an animal in order to lead it to life-giving water. This gives a simple but powerful principle for us to follow here. Once all the spiritual *bondage* has been released we can come to the Lord for spiritual, emotional and physical *healing* for all that has been damaged through the ungodly control. Without the ungodly yoke, our bodies can at last straighten up!

A suggestion for what to say:

Father God, thank you for setting me free from the bondage of control. I seek restoration and healing for my whole body, soul and spirit. Where fear has gripped me, I ask for Your love to fill my heart. Where control has crushed me, I ask for Your strength to help me rise up. Where infirmity has weakened me, I ask for Your healing to restore me.

Thank you that You release prisoners and You bind up the broken-hearted. I choose to walk forward in freedom and wholeness, in Jesus mighty name.

Step 8. Identify roots of wounding and insecurity which led to the use of ungodly control.

Lastly, we need to remember that controlling behavior is always a symptom of a deeper issue; it's a sinful response to inner wounding. If we have resorted to control in our relationships we must recognize that there will be a need to find the roots of damage which led to the controlling behavior. There may have been rejection, abuse, betrayal, abandonment or trauma.

As God reveals the wounded places we can choose to forgive those who hurt us and receive His comfort, His acceptance and His healing at this deeper level. We can confidently declare that it's God's control over our lives which provides the true remedy and no longer the ungodly forms of control which we thought would alleviate the pain.

A suggestion for what to say:

Father God, You see deep into the roots of why control has been a part of my life. I learned and used these controlling behaviors to guard the hurting and insecure places inside me. I thought that I alone needed to take control of my life and all my relationships. Now I surrender this control to You and welcome you into my wounded heart. I forgive . . . (Name those who sinned against you) and receive Your perfect comfort, healing and protection, in the name of my Lord and Savior Jesus.

Summary

Knowing truth is valuable. Applying that truth is life-changing. We can bring to God the issues which He reveals in our lives and discover amazing steps of freedom and wholeness as we confess our own sin and forgive those who have sinned against us.

Prayer is listening to God's truth and to His commands and then speaking our response. As we agree with Him, the enemy's hold on our lives is disabled and we can expel him. We then discover Holy Spirit power to walk in a new place of freedom and wholeness.

As we realize how damaging ungodly control can be within God's family, how do we encourage godly authority and power without condoning sinful controlling behavior? We shall explore this question now in the final chapter.

CHAPTER 10

Leading Without Ungodly Control

Understanding headship

The human body doesn't do well without a head. The brain gathers vital information from every part of our being and directs the body to act in an appropriate way. As our fingers touch the world around us, they provide some of this important information advising on what is hard or soft, hot or cold. Our hands respond to the directions of the brain in a multitude of essential tasks such as holding, carrying and defending. The interdependence and order within the body is essential for our well-being; each part fitting into the order of the whole, without claiming inappropriate precedence.

The Bible tells us that this same order is essential for the rightful functioning of the Godhead and for mankind. Paul summarizes this foundational principle by describing the order of authority (or headship) which flows down from the Father, through Jesus, to a man and his wife.

> *But I would have you know, that the head of every man is Christ; and the head of the woman is the man; and the head of Christ is God.*
>
> 1 Corinthians 11:3, KJV

It's not an issue of status. It's an issue of order. Jesus was fully aware of His equality with the Father but He also knew the necessity of a divine protocol for the fulfillment of God's plans for mankind.

The attitude you should have is the one that Christ Jesus had: He always had the nature of God, but he did not think that by force he should try to remain equal with God. Instead of this, of his own free will he gave up all he had, and took the nature of a servant. He became like a human being and appeared in human likeness.

Philippians 2:5-7, GNB

Someone needs to lead

We looked earlier at the situation on an airplane. We're very happy that the pilot assumes control because he's under a right authority, which has released him to fly the plane. The headship is clear. He has those in authority *over* him back at company headquarters and a whole planeload of people content to be *under* his authority. The boundaries of the pilot's rightful control are clear. He doesn't tell his passengers which in-flight movie to watch or what food to eat. That authority hasn't been delegated to him.

Throughout the Bible we see God directing his people through the delegation of leadership to particular individuals such as Moses, Joshua and the judges. They are far from perfect people but they're selected by God for the task of giving direction and they're supported by others who are there to bring some of God's wisdom. Moses would have preferred a different choice but God had decided to choose him as a leader and the main support was to be Aaron.

But Moses said, "No, LORD, don't send me. I have never been a good speaker, and I haven't become one since you began to speak to me. I am a poor speaker, slow and hesitant." The LORD said to him, "Who gives man his mouth? Who makes him deaf or dumb? Who gives him sight or makes him blind? It is I, the LORD. Now, go! I will help you to speak, and I will tell you what to say."

Exodus 4:10-12, GNB

Paul reminds us that God chooses people in just the same way today and He equips them to carry His authority in all of the tasks of shepherding the Body of Christ. Paul encourages each of us to get on with the job, not least those called to take the lead.

> *For even as we have many members in one body, but all members do not have the same function, so we the many are one body in Christ, and each one members of one another, but having different gifts according to the grace given to us, whether prophecy, according to the proportion of the faith; or ministry, in the ministry; or the one teaching, in the teaching or the one exhorting, in the encouragement; the one sharing, in simplicity; the one taking the lead, in diligence; the one showing mercy, in cheerfulness.*
>
> Romans 12:4-8, LITV

Those to whom leadership authority has been delegated are encouraged in this passage to *'take the lead in diligence'*. We could translate this even more literally as *'if you are called to stand at the front and give direction, get on with it!'* And yet so often we shy away from godly leadership in the Body of Christ. Why is this? Let's look at the alternatives.

Dictatorship is one option!

Under this system one person takes control, by his or her own authority, and in many nations around the world this is enabled by military force. Things often happen fast under such rule as very little discussion is encouraged. The directions given may be very clear but this leadership is ultimately ungodly, because there has been neither rightful delegation of authority nor has there usually been any free will choice by those being ruled.

Spiritually, dictatorship is enemy territory. We frequently see dictators, who may have started with some noble intentions, descend into barbaric domination of the people, showing many of the destructive characteristics of Satan, the ruler of this world. When a self-styled leader is not under right authority he will increasingly exercise demonic control. The result of this type of leadership can be increasing corruption of all kinds. God strongly discouraged His people from abandoning judges in favor of kings. Kings tend to elevate themselves rather than God. Dictatorship is not God's way for His church.

Democracy can seem a good option

In trying to avoid the oppression of dictatorship, most nations in the world have seen democracy as the safest form of rule. In this system the authority and power (or control) is given to the group who're in the majority. Theoretically, it is rule by the people, but those with persuasive skills (adept in controlling techniques) can very often manipulate the voters to get the majority on their side. This may be evident in national elections but it can be even more apparent in a church meeting where the disapproval of just one intimidating participant can sway the group.

Democracy does indeed present a better alternative to dictatorship, especially at national level, but there's very little evidence in the Bible of it being God's way for the leading of His people. The disciples certainly drew lots to determine who was going to replace Judas. However this wasn't carried out with persuasive debate but by waiting on the personal direction of God through prayer, once Peter had taken a clear lead in presenting the matter.

> *Then they prayed, "Lord, you know the thoughts of everyone, so show us which of these two you have chosen to serve as an apostle in the place of Judas, who left to go to the place where he belongs."*
> Acts 1:24-25, GNB

As soon as we encourage the taking of *sides* in any meeting which has been called to discover God's way forward, there's always the opportunity for the enemy to use one of his power tools – *division*. Of course, different opinions can and should be freely expressed, but if it's the majority that will win the day we may find ourselves working harder to gain the support of others rather than really determining the will of God. Through fear of ungodly control, many churches opt for democratic procedures, but does this really encourage the seeking of God's wisdom or does it just foster the art of human persuasion?

In the Body of Christ, we must ask ourselves some questions. Is it God's way to always impart His wisdom to the majority in any meeting? Whilst views should certainly be expressed, can democratic debate, to form a majority, actually dilute the destiny which God has purposed for His people? God progresses His purposes through revelation, which should be received, weighed and tested through prayer. Are we better to discern and pray for those whom God is using to bring revelation and direction, rather than demanding the right to vote?

I suggest that democracy in the church may miss God's best.

Surely consensus must be the right way

In this system, no decision is taken until everyone agrees. It sounds so very fair, but it ignores the reality of our sinful human nature. In an ideal world, if we all had the fullness of the purity of Jesus, we would all agree with the guidance of the Holy Spirit and therefore agree with each other. But we're damaged vessels living in a fallen world and we're still very capable of sin and selfishness.

Here's one definition of consensus: *a way of reaching a decision by striving to find a broad-based agreement by all participants.* If we wait to make a decision which contradicts nobody's viewpoint, we will surely water down the radical directions of God. Not all will have the same enthusiasm to take risks in moving on with God. Not all will see clearly the vision for what God has planned. We will normally only find a consensus for the *safest* option and this can be a recipe for stagnation.

Once again human eloquence and persuasive ability may well prove to be the most significant instruments in reaching a consensus. A phrase from Acts 15 is often quoted: '*it seemed good to us and the Holy Spirit*'. This is certainly an excellent definition of godly agreement, but we should note that the brethren in this particular meeting were actually choosing to acknowledge and to follow the leadership, and a decision, of James.

> *After they had stopped speaking, James answered, saying, "Brethren, listen to me... it is my judgment that we do not trouble those who are turning to God from among the Gentile..."*
>
> Acts 15:13, 19, NAS

The word *judgment* here means to make a decision based on the evidence submitted. James recognized within himself God's gifting to give direction. The others in the meeting chose to recognize and submit to that authority. This wasn't rule by consensus but a willingness by all in the group to acknowledge the gifting of the person *through whom* God was revealing His way forward. James led and the others (by a free-will choice) clearly decided it was right to follow him. James was acting in a similar way to the judges of the Old Testament.

If we're not careful, waiting for consensus can deny the dynamic potential of godly authority and power.

God's way of leading His people

The Holy Spirit distributes different gifting to each individual for the benefit of the whole body of believers. We shouldn't all expect to have the same measure of revelation or faith for a particular situation, but we can benefit from that which God has given to others. Some will be equipped to teach with wisdom, some to bring revelation or faith, some to hear God's voice and some to weigh the information and give clear direction.

God's way of leading His people is through the principle of headship. We are encouraged to see ourselves as a living body. Information flows to and from the head (the one who gives direction), with every part of the body recognizing the distinctive gifting and wisdom of the various members. When all the information has been exchanged, the body allows the head to give direction. I will repeat what has been written earlier in this book. Godly authority is not a matter of status but of right order. Brain activity in our head is dependent for oxygen on the heart, but the heart only continues pumping under the direction of the brain. Every human body needs a head. Every group of God's people, whether it's a family or a church, needs a clear leader, operating *under* and *in* godly authority and power. In a violent storm, the captain of a ship, having listened to the advice of the experienced members of the crew, must make and stand by his decision as to which direction to take.

Praying for each member of the body, particularly the head (the leader), will prove so much more powerful than disapproval. When God establishes His order within the Body of Christ, He also equips each member. It has often been said that those He *appoints* He also *anoints*. Seeking this structure of godly order and authority brings both safety and dynamic advancement of God's Kingdom. God will cover genuine mistakes where there's godly authority, leadership and submission; He can't cover willful rebellion.

It's not easy to be a godly leader. There's a very narrow path between wrong control on the one side and wrong abdication on the other. Leaders need to exercise authority in a way that doesn't threaten, intimidate, manipulate or coerce. Neither should they draw back from the responsibility of giving strong direction. Nor should they fail, at the right time, to confront wrong behavior amongst those whom they're leading. Godly leaders show clear direction and clear boundaries to those who follow, but godly leaders also give complete freedom for their followers to choose whether they wish walk the same path.

Dealing with a legacy of ungodly control in the church

In many of our churches there remains an unresolved spiritual legacy of Jezebel control. This needs to be seriously considered by the whole church, and especially by leaders, if they really want to walk in godly order and authority. When past sin of ungodly control hasn't been acknowledged and dealt with, churches can find themselves struggling with an unclean spiritual inheritance. Land, buildings and communities become spiritually defiled by the unresolved sin of those who have previously occupied the same ground.

> *Do not make yourselves unclean by any of these acts, for that is how the pagans made themselves unclean, those pagans who lived in the land before you and whom the LORD is driving out so that you can go in. Their actions made the land unclean, and so the LORD is punishing the land and making it reject the people who lived there.*
> Leviticus 18:24-25, GNB

Sin, past or present, is not dealt with by sweeping it under the carpet. If we honestly confess our sin, and the sin of those who have been part of the church before us, then God will cleanse the demonic powers which seek to rule over the church, not least in the area of Jezebel control. We saw in the story of Queen Jezebel that a primary purpose of this spirit was to destroy godly order and authority. God hates the work of this spirit and the defiled inheritance in Ahab's family line was removed by the destruction of the entire family.

Thankfully, Jesus has paid the penalty now for the sin of each one of us and we can find freedom individually and corporately by forgiving those who have sown sinful control into our church family, and by confessing our own sin. It has always been a covenant promise of God that both people and land are cleansed through the acknowledgement of iniquity.

> *If they confess their iniquity and the iniquity of their forefathers, in their unfaithfulness which they committed against Me, and also in their acting with hostility against Me.... then I will remember My covenant with Jacob, and I will remember also My covenant with Isaac, and My covenant with Abraham as well, and I will remember the land.*
> Leviticus 26:40, 42, NAS

When God is given full authority over our church through such prayers, we can address the ruling spirits of the enemy and expel them from our fellowship and our places of worship. Ellel Ministries has witnessed dramatic freedom for congregations, caught up in Jezebel control issues, when this legacy from the past has been clearly addressed.

Last thoughts

Control is the combination of authority and power. For many people, control is a dirty word, with unpleasant associations. In the hands of the enemy it certainly is a very dirty practice. At creation, God delegated to mankind spiritual authority and power in order to demonstrate His character throughout His creation. Satan has been handed this authority through the rebellion against God which has been in each one of us. Through Jesus Christ, we have an amazing opportunity to claim the authority back and once again demonstrate God's fruitfulness.

We can only exercise right authority and power when we're under right authority. Ungodly control occurs when we assume our own authority or act on behalf of others who're in rebellion to God. We use wrong control for many reasons but mostly because we believe that it will bring security or significance. It doesn't work because it destroys true relationship.

Most of us have experienced all the facets of control, both sinning and being sinned against. Jesus was able to walk in complete freedom despite all the abuse that was directed towards Him. He invites us to walk into the same freedom, knowing the supernatural authority and power of God without the defiling control of the enemy, which has trapped so many people. In safe hands, godly control directs and protects without doing any harm. We have a unique opportunity as Christians to experience and promote a radical alternative to the manipulative lifestyles which have become so ingrained in the ways of this world and even in the church.

Jesus has been given supreme authority over all of creation on earth and in heaven. Despite this, He allows us complete freedom to reject Him or to follow Him. He makes clear His unconditional love for us but He will never manipulate, intimidate or coerce us into loving Him. If that's His desired relationship with us, surely we should seek to establish the same in all our relationships with each other. This *is* possible in Christ Jesus.

About Ellel Ministries

Our Vision

Ellel Ministries is a non-denominational Christian Mission Organization with a vision to resource and equip the Church by welcoming people, teaching them about the Kingdom of God and healing those in need (Luke 9:11).

Our Mission

Our mission is to fulfill the above vision throughout the world, as God opens the doors, in accordance with the Great Commission of Jesus and the calling of the Church to proclaim the Kingdom of God by preaching the good news, healing the broken-hearted and setting the captives free. We are, therefore, committed to evangelism, healing, deliverance, discipleship and training. The particular scriptures on which our mission is founded are Isaiah 61:1–7; Matthew 28:18–20; Luke 9:1–2; 9:11; Ephesians 4:12; 2 Timothy 2:2.

Our Basis of Faith

God is a Trinity. God the Father loves all people. God the Son, Jesus Christ, is Savior and Healer, Lord and King. God the Holy Spirit indwells Christians and imparts the dynamic power by which they are enabled to continue Christ's ministry. The Bible is the divinely inspired authority in matters of faith, doctrine and conduct, and is the basis for teaching.

For more information

Please visit our website at www.ellelministries.org for full up-to-date information about the world-wide work of Ellel Ministries.

Ellel Ministries Centers

International Head Office

Ellel Grange
Ellel, Lancaster LA2 0HN, UK
t: +44 (0) 1524 751651
f: +44 (0) 1524 751738
e: info.grange@ellelministries.org

Ellel Glyndley Manor
Stone Cross, Pevensey, E. Sussex
BN24 5BS, UK
t: +44 (0) 1323 440440
f: +44 (0) 1323 440877
e: info.glyndley@ellelministries.org

Ellel Pierrepont
Frensham, Farnham, Surrey
GU10 3DL, UK
t: +44 (0) 1252 794060
f: +44 (0) 1252 794039
e: info.pierrepont@ellelministries.org

Ellel Scotland
Blairmore House, Glass, Huntly,
Aberdeenshire AB54 4XH, Scotland
t: +44 (0) 1466 799102
f: +44 (0) 1466 700205
e: info.scotland@ellelministries.org

Ellel Ministries Ireland
35 Beanstown Road, Lisburn, County Antrim,
BT28 3QS, Northern Ireland
t: +44 (0) 28 9260 7162
e: info.northernireland@ellelministries.org

Ellel Ministries Africa
PO Box 39569, Faerie Glen 0043, Pretoria,
South Africa
t: +27 (0) 12 809 0031/1172
f: +27 12 809 1173
e: info.africa@ellelministries.org

Ellel Ministries Australia (Sydney)
Gilbulla, 710 Moreton Park Road, Menangle,
2568, NSW, Australia
t: +61 (02) 4633 8102
f: +61 (02) 4633 8201
e: info.gilbulla@ellelministries.org

Ellel Ministries Australia Headquarters (Perth)
Springhill, PO Box 609, Northam, WA, 6401, Australia
t: +61 (08) 9622 5568
f: +61 (08) 9622 5123
e: info.springhill@ellelministries.org

Ellel Ministries Canada Derbyshire Downs
183 Hanna Rd., RR#2, Westport, Ontario, K0G 1X0, Canada
t: +1 (613) 273 8700
e: info.ontario@ellelministries.org

Ellel Ministries Canada West
10-5918 5 St SE, Calgary, Alberta, T2H 1L4, Canada
t: +1 (403) 238 2008
f: +1 (866) 246 5918
e: info.calgary@ellelministries.org

Ellel Ministries France (Fraternité Chrétienne)
10 Avenue Jules Ferry, 38380 Saint Laurent du Pont, France
t: +33 (0) 476 554 266
e: info.france@ellelministries.org

Ellel Ministries Germany
Bahnhoffstr. 43-47, 72213 Altensteig, Deutschland
w: www.ellelgermany.de
t: +49 (0) 7453 275 51
e: info.germany@ellelministries.org

Ellel Ministries Hungary
Veresegyház, PF17, 2112, Hungary
t/f: +36 28 362396
e: info.hungary@ellelministries.org

Ellel Central & Eastern Europe Development
Veresegyház, PF17, 2112, Hungary
t: +36 28 362410 / f: +36 28 362396
e: info.regionalnations@ellelministries.org

Ellel India
502, Orchid, Holy Cross Road, IC Colony, Borivli West, Mumbai 400 103, India
mobile: +91 (0) 93 2224 5209
e: info.india@ellelministries.org

Ellel Ministries Malaysia
Lot 2, Ground and 1st Floor, Wisma Leven Lorong Margosa 2, Luyang Phase 8, 88300 Kota Kinabalu, Sabah, Malaysia
t: +6088 270246
f: +6088 270280
e: info.malaysia@ellelministries.org

Ellel Ministries Netherlands
Wichmondseweg 19, 7223 LH Baak, Netherlands
t: +31 575 441452
e: info.netherlands@ellelministries.org

Ellel Ministries New Zealand
info.newzealand@ellelministries.org

Ellel Ministries Norway
Stiftelsen Ellel Ministries Norge, Hogstveien 2, 2006 Løvenstad, Norge (Norway)
t: +47 67413150
e: info.norway@ellelministries.org

Ellel Ministries Singapore
Thomson Post Office, PO Box 204, Singapore 915707
t: +65 6252 4234
f: +65 6252 3792
e: info.singapore@ellelministries.org

Ellel Ministries Sweden
Kvarnbackavägen 4 B, 711 92 Vedevåg, Sweden
t: +46 581 93140
e: info.sweden@ellelministries.org

Ellel Ministries USA
1708 English Acres Drive, Lithia, Florida, 33547, USA
t: +1 (813) 737 4848
f: +1 (813) 737 9051
e: info.usa@ellelministries.org

*All details are correct at time of going to press (November 2012) but are subject to change.

Ellel Ministries' Truth & Freedom Series Books

Available in eBook formats

Soul Ties
The Unseen Bond in Relationships
By David Cross

Intercession & Healing
Breaking through with God
By Fional Horrobin

Sex, God's Truth
By Jill Southern

Trapped by Control
How to Find Freedom
By David Cross

Stepping Stones to the Father Heart of God
By Margaret Silvester

Anger
How Do You Handle It?
By Paul & Liz Griffin

Hope & Healing for the Abused
By Paul & Liz Griffin

Rescue from Rejection
Finding Security in God's Loving Acceptance
By Denise Cross

God's Covering
A Place of Healing
By David Cross

The Dangers of Alternative Ways to Healing
How to Avoid the New Age Deception
By David Cross & John Berry

About the Author

David Cross directs the Ellel Ministries' team based at Glyndley Manor, a center for Christian teaching and restoration, which is situated near Eastbourne on the south coast of England. He qualified as a civil engineer but developed many life skills in a most varied working career, which included leading ski-tours in the Scottish Highlands. Despite fulfillment at work David found himself gradually more and more disillusioned with the ethos of "self sufficiency" on which he had based his life up until that point.

A change in direction came when he was converted in Hong Kong in the early 1980s and he eagerly began to follow Jesus. On returning to the UK in 1984 he became an elder in the Church of Scotland. Then in 1993, he and his wife Denise joined Ellel Ministries. David's clear and authoritative teaching from God's Word has brought understanding and healing to many who have been confused and damaged by the ideologies of today's world.

David has written two books in the Truth & Freedom series published by Sovereign World, *Soul Ties: The Unseen Bond in Relationships* and *God's Covering: A Place of Healing.*

We hope you enjoyed reading this
Sovereign World book.
For more details of other
books and new releases see our website:

www.sovereignworld.com

Find us on:
Twitter @sovereignworld
Like us on:
www.facebook.com/sovereignworld

Our authors welcome your feedback on their books.
Please send your comments to our offices.
You can request to subscribe to
our email and mailing list online or by writing to:

Sovereign World Ltd, PO Box 784,
Ellel, Lancaster, LA1 9DA, United Kingdom
info@sovereignworld.com

Sovereign World titles are available from
all good Christian bookshops and eBook vendors.

For information about our distributors in the UK,
USA, Canada, South Africa, Australia and Singapore, visit:
www.sovereignworld.com/trade

If you would like to help us send a copy of this book and
many other titles to needy pastors in developing countries,
please write for further information or send your gift to:

Sovereign World Trust, PO Box 777,
Tonbridge, Kent TN11 0ZS
United Kingdom
www.sovereignworldtrust.org.uk

The Sovereign World Trust is a registered charity

CPSIA information can be obtained at www.ICGtesting.com
Printed in the USA
LVOW08s0227230615

443481LV00024B/380/P